# Flower Nature

## Colouring Book

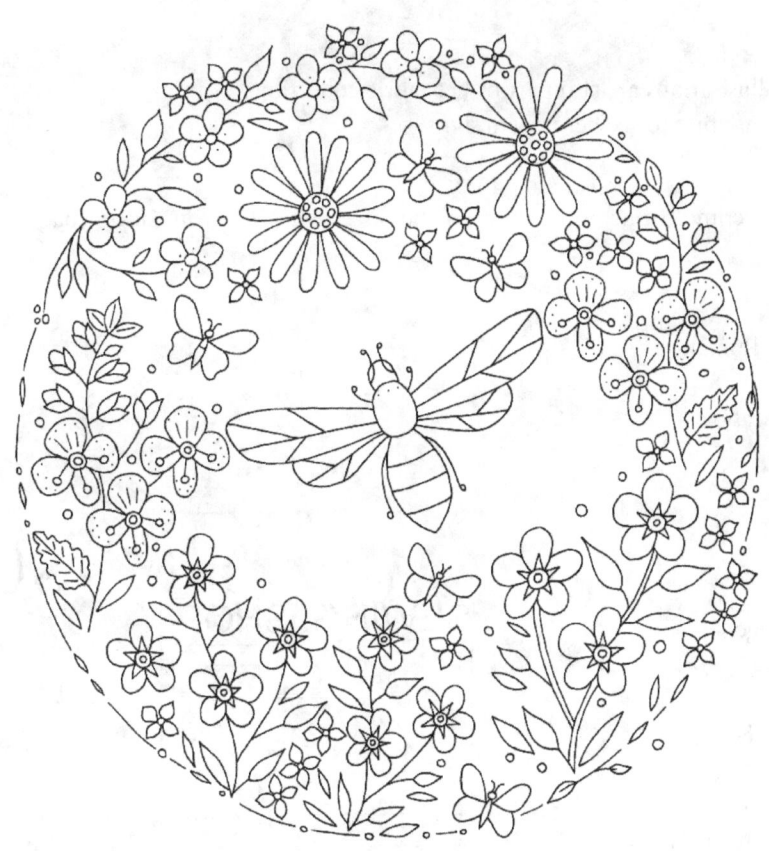

## De-ann Black

Published 2020

ISBN: 9798685712875

**Colouring books** by De-ann Black: Summer Garden, Sea Dream, Flower Bee, Bee Garden, Flower Hunter, Autumn Garden, Christmas Garden, Festive Christmas, Wild Garden, Faerie Garden Spring, Stargazer Space, Spring Garden and Scottish Garden Seasons. Her embroidery books, Floral Nature Embroidery Designs and Scottish Garden Embroidery Designs are also available.

Further details about De-ann's books, art, illustrations and fabric designs are available from her website - www.De-annBlack.com

**Fabric Designs**
De-ann's artwork and illustrations are also part of her fabric collections.
Go to De-annBlack.com/fabric to see her new designs.

**Fiction Books**
De-ann writes romance, crime/thrillers and children's books. See her Amazon Author page or website for her latest books.

**Romance:**
The Sewing Shop
Heather Park: Regency Romance
The Tea Shop by the Sea
The Bookshop by the Seaside
The Sewing Bee
The Quilting Bee
Snow Bells Wedding
Snow Bells Christmas
Summer Sewing Bee
The Chocolatier's Cottage
Christmas Cake Chateau
The Beemaster's Cottage
The Sewing Bee By The Sea
The Flower Hunter's Cottage
The Christmas Knitting Bee
The Sewing Bee & Afternoon Tea
The Tea Shop
Shed In The City
The Bakery By The Seaside
Champagne Chic Lemonade Money
The Christmas Chocolatier
The Christmas Tea Shop & Bakery
Dublin Girl - Hot Summer In The City
Oops! I'm The Paparazzi
The Cure For Love

**Crime/Thrillers:**
Love Him Forever
Someone Worse
Electric Shadows
The Strife Of Riley

**Children's books:**
Faeriefied
Secondhand Spooks
Poison-Wynd
Science Fashion
Wormhole Wynd

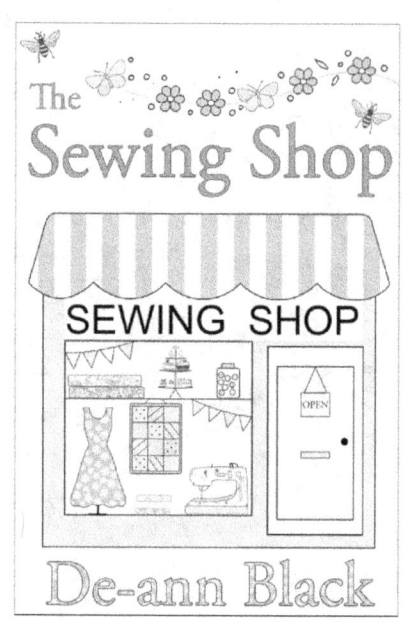

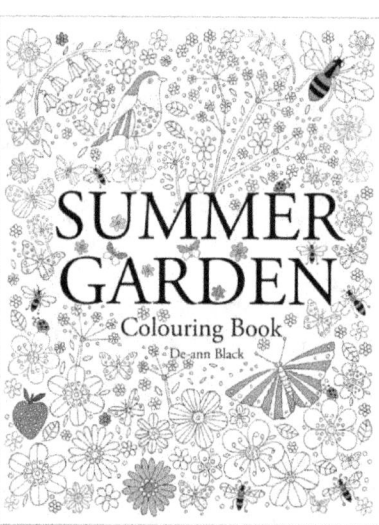

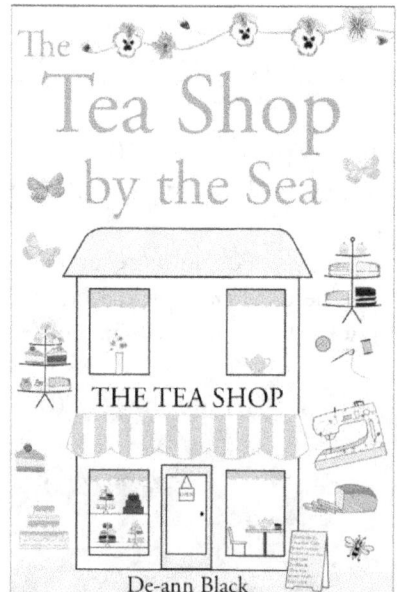

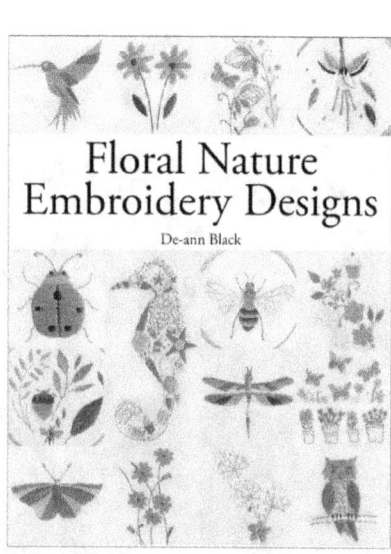

De-ann Black is a bestselling author, scriptwriter and former newspaper journalist. She has over 80 books published. She's also an artist and fabric designer.

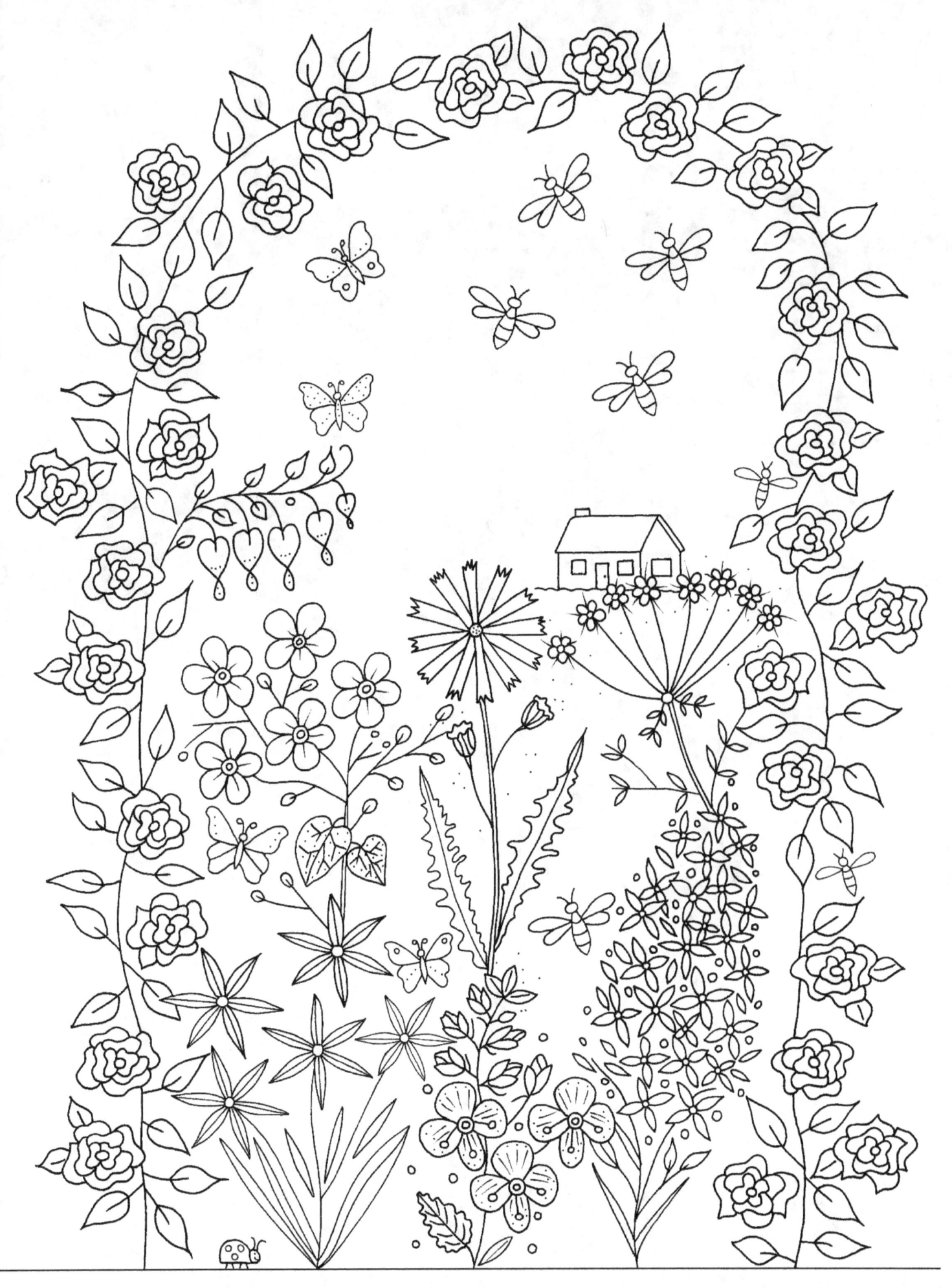

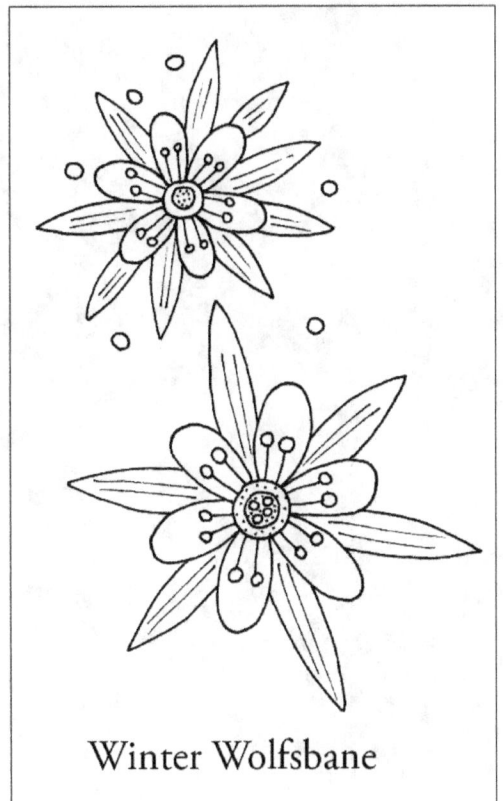

Winter Wolfsbane

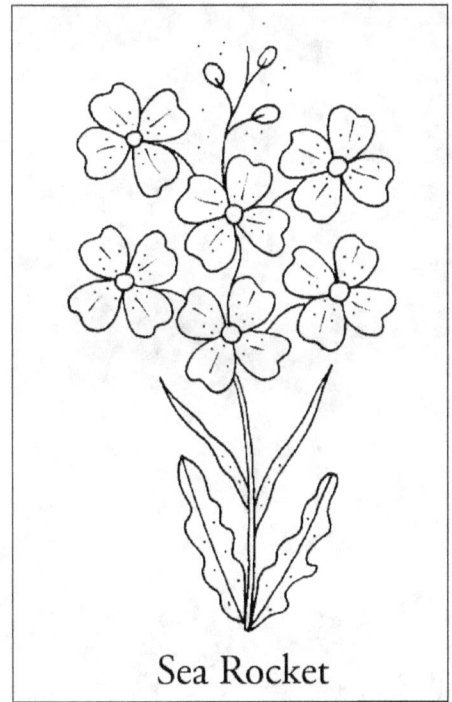

Sea Rocket

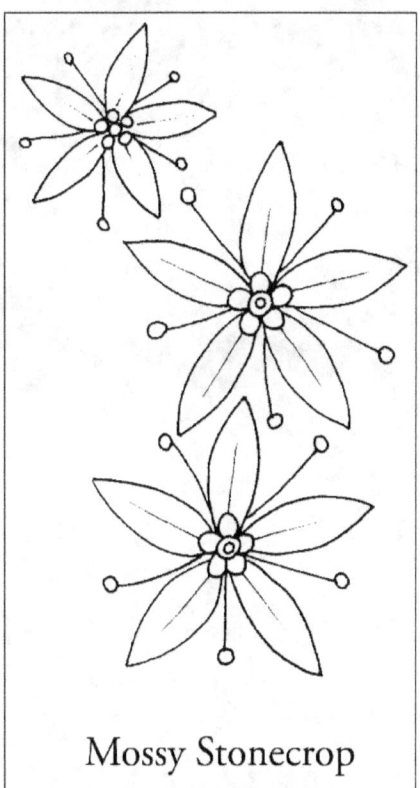

Mossy Stonecrop

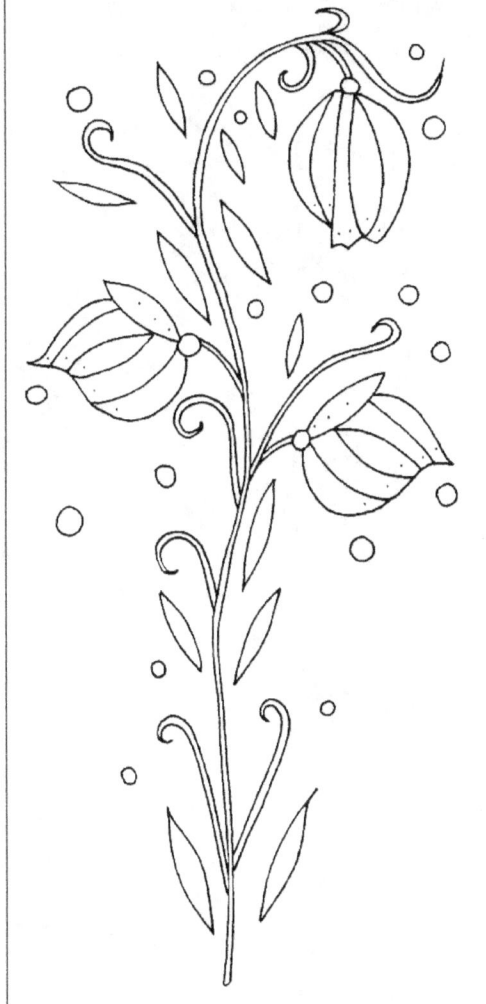

Fairy Lantern Flowers

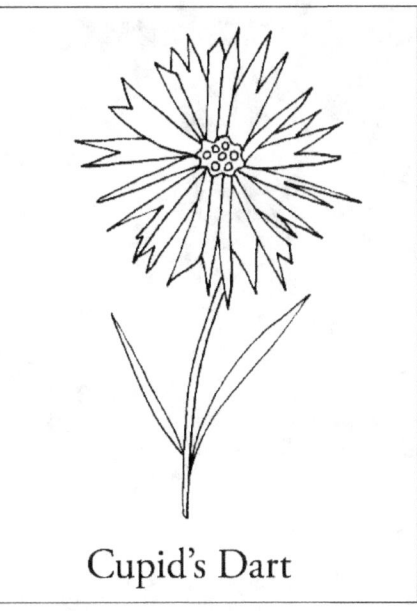

Cupid's Dart

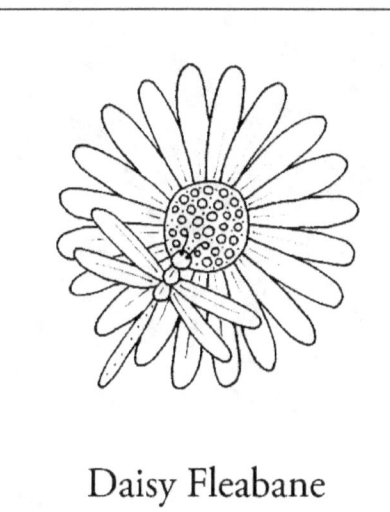

Daisy Fleabane

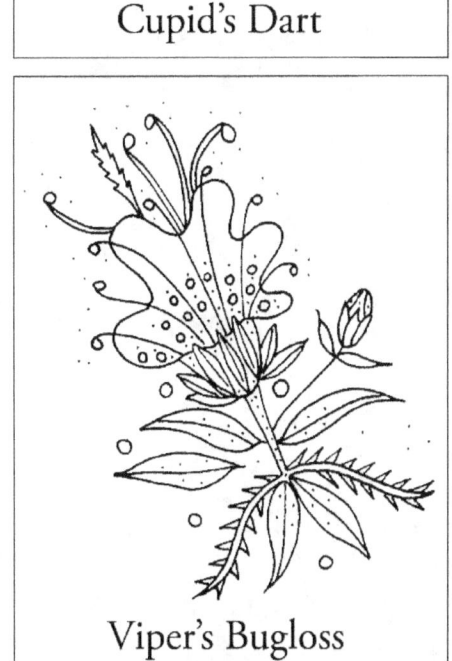

Viper's Bugloss

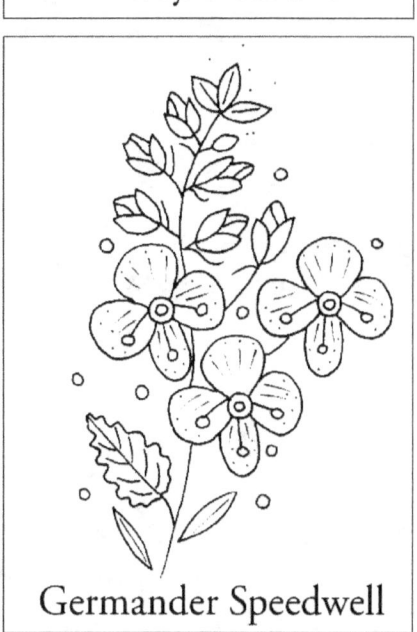

Germander Speedwell

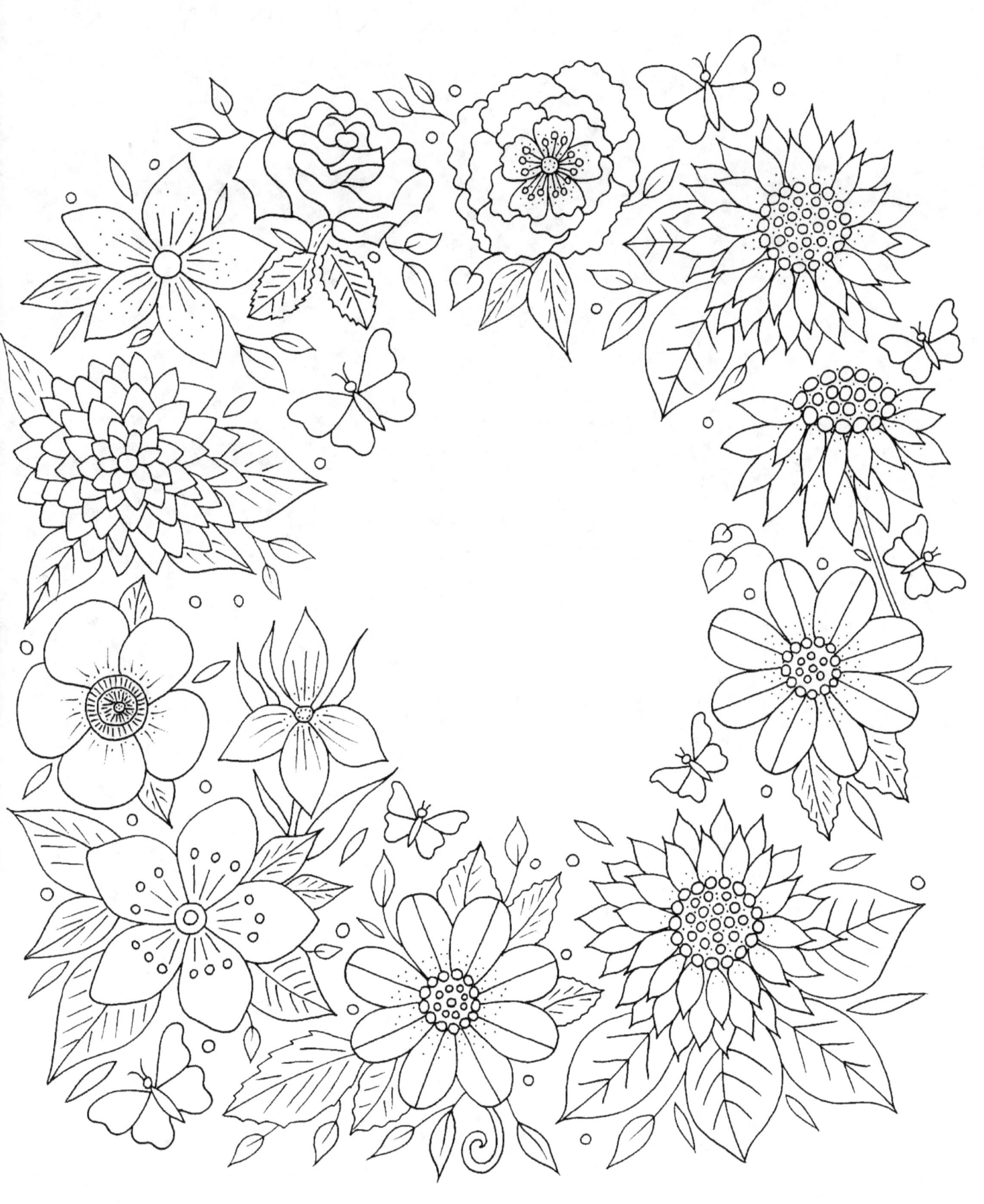

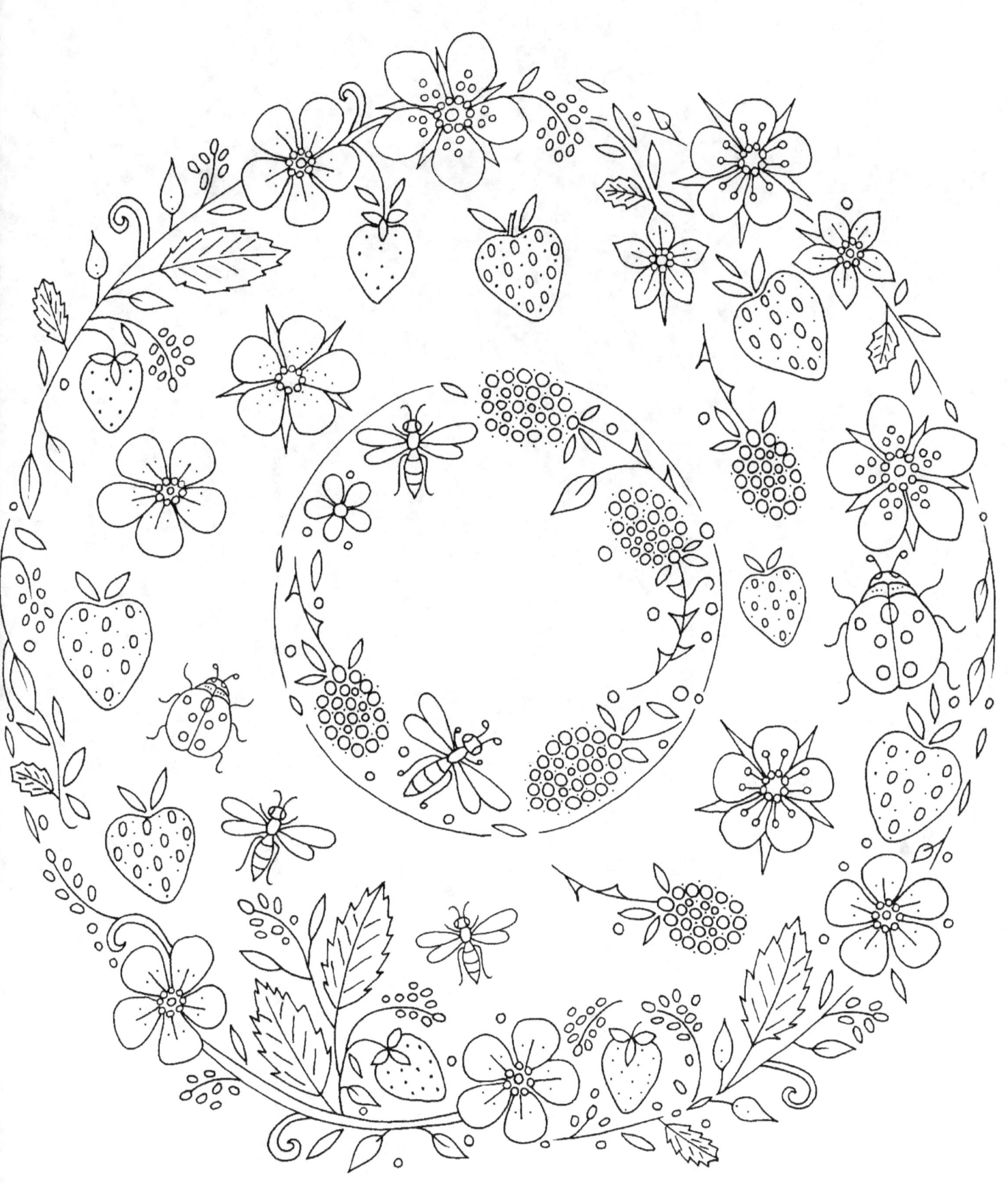

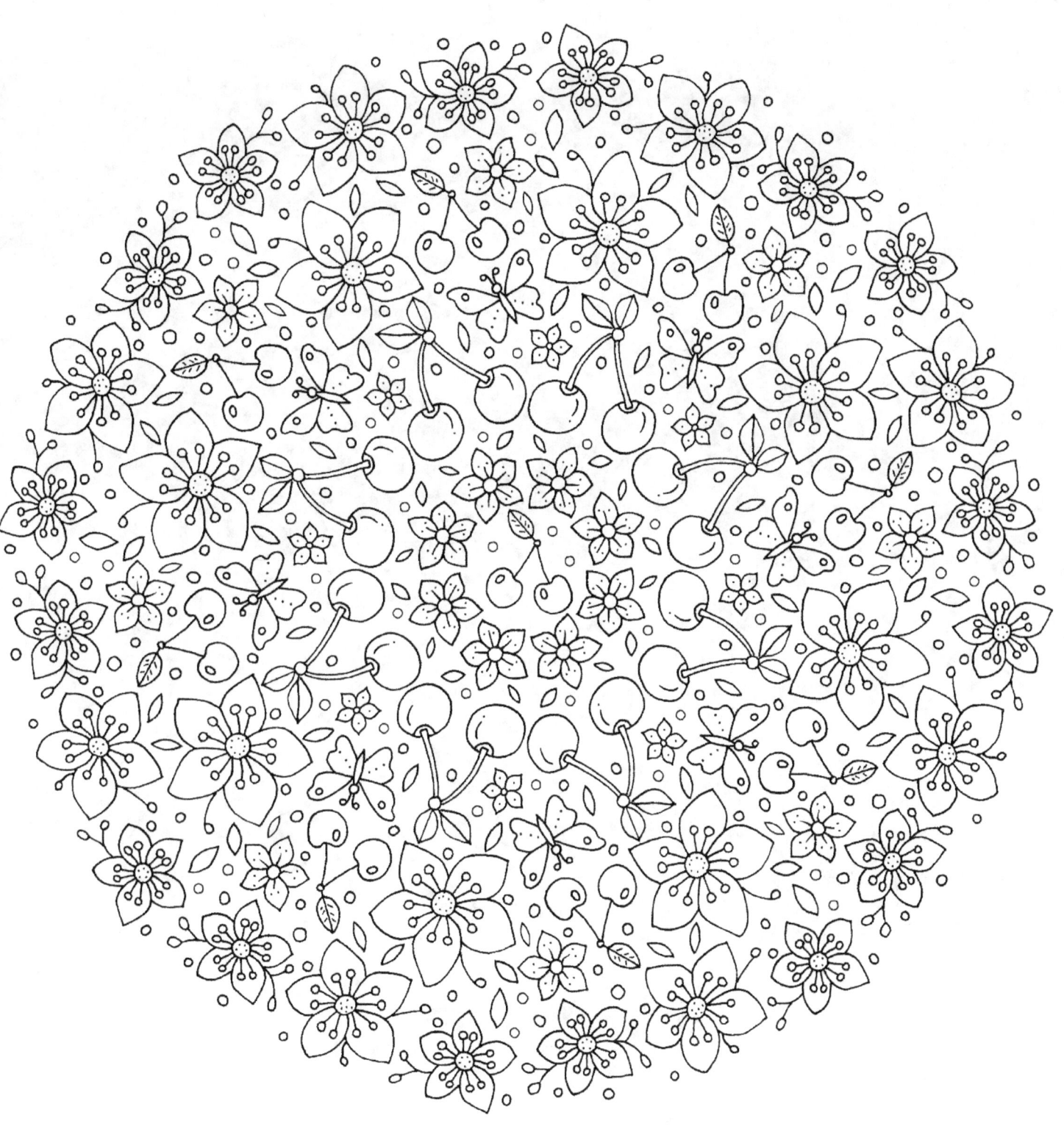

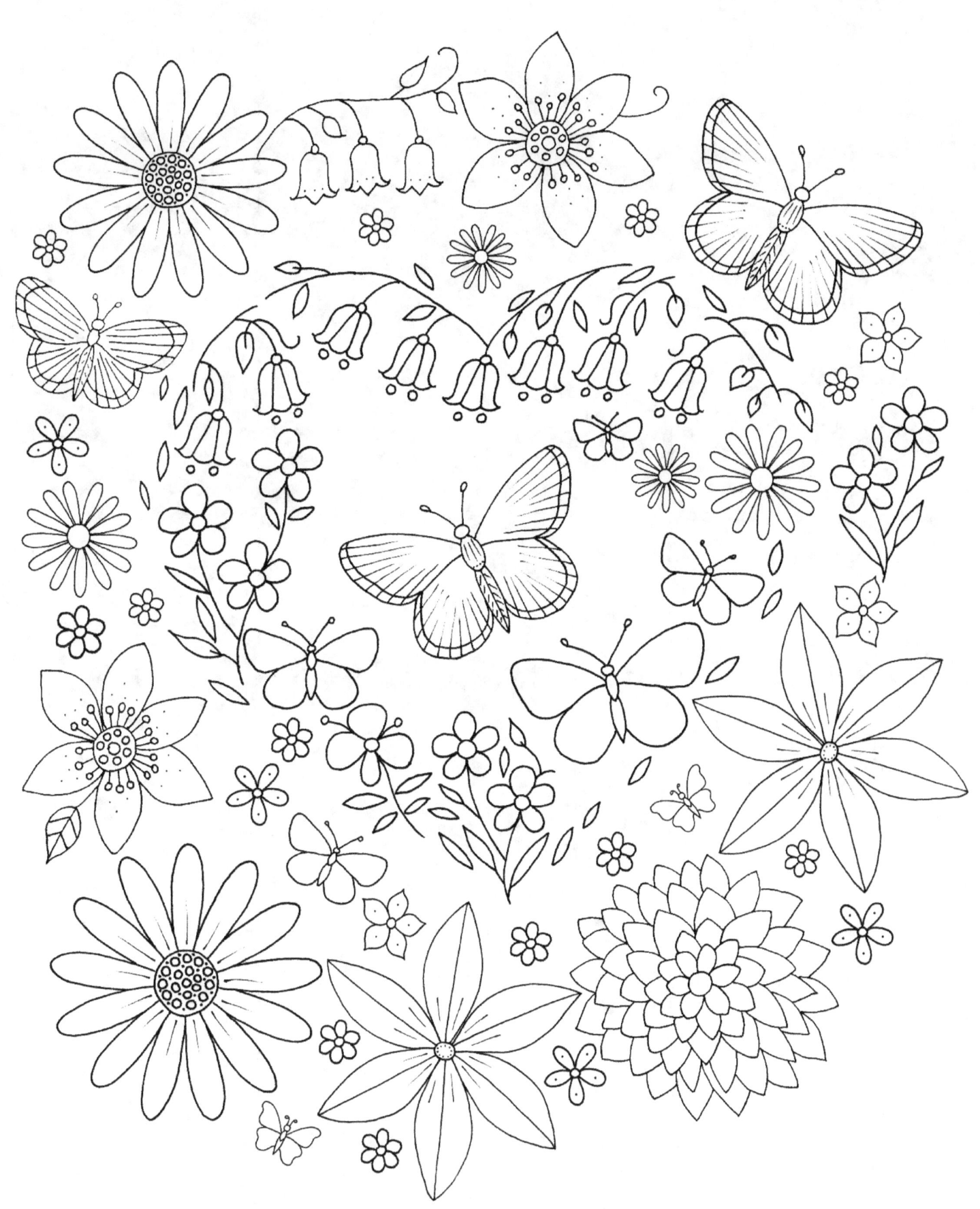

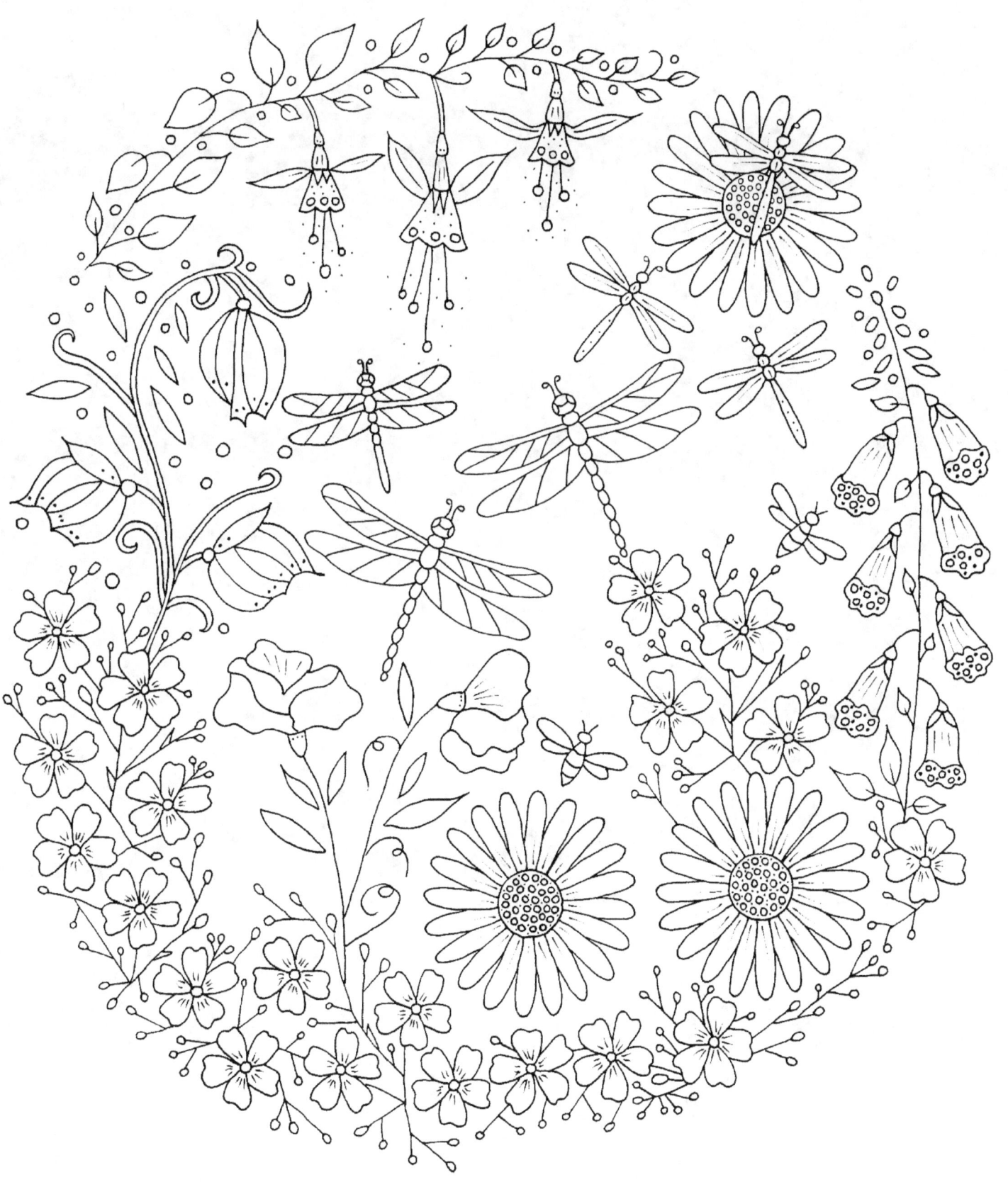

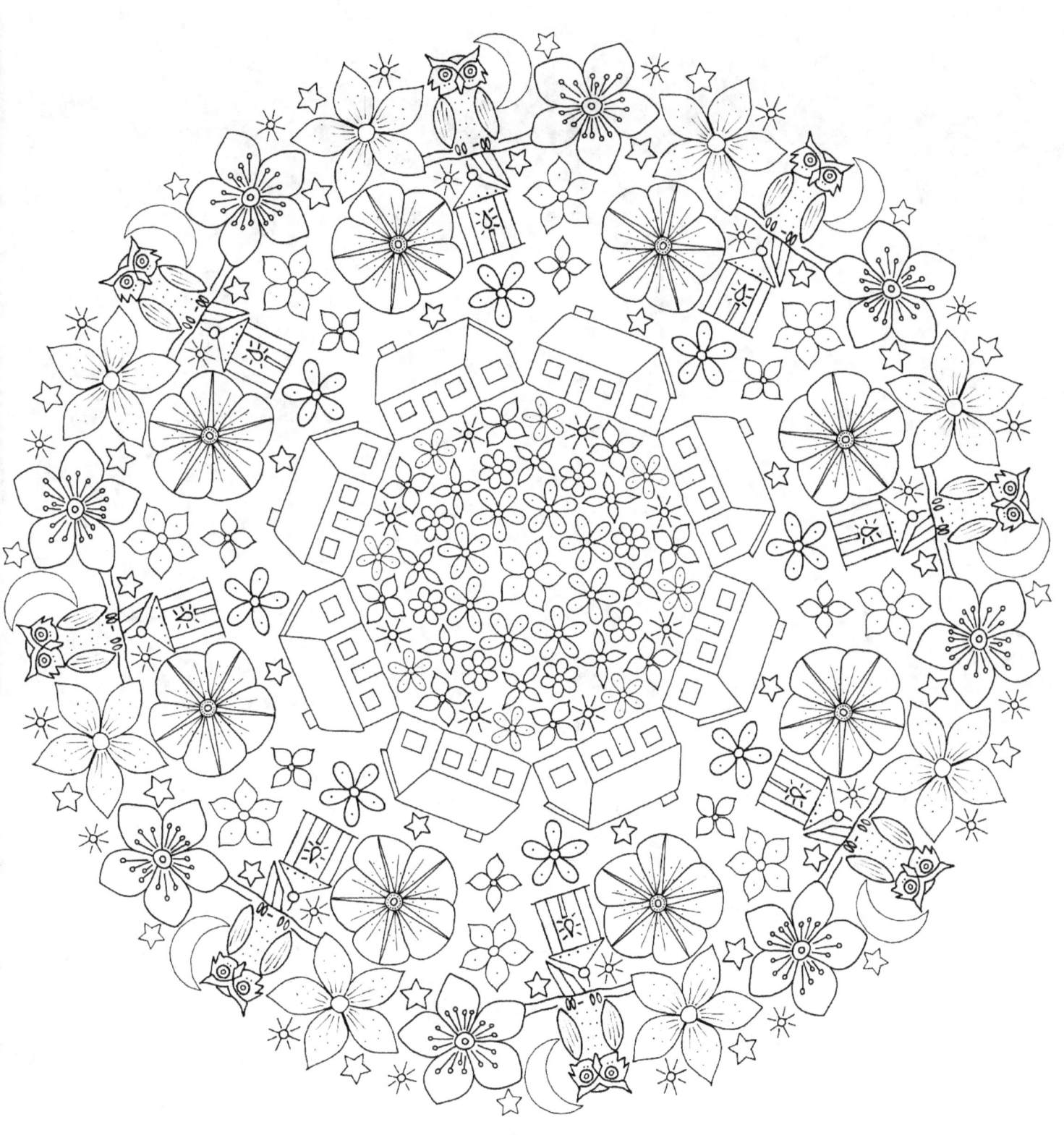

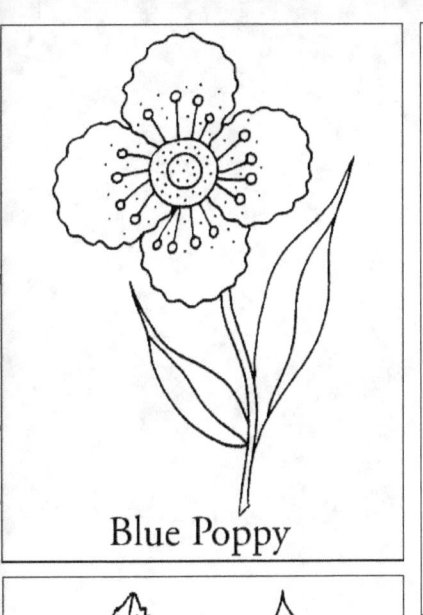

Blue Poppy

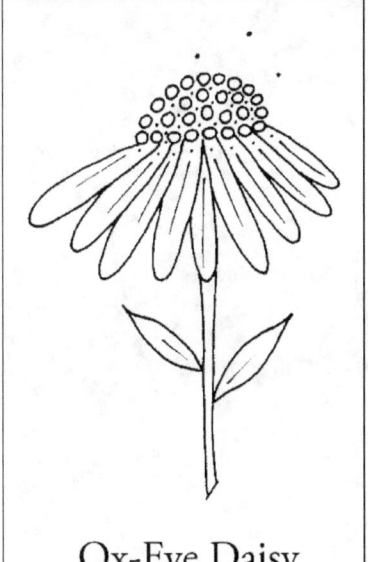

Ox-Eye Daisy

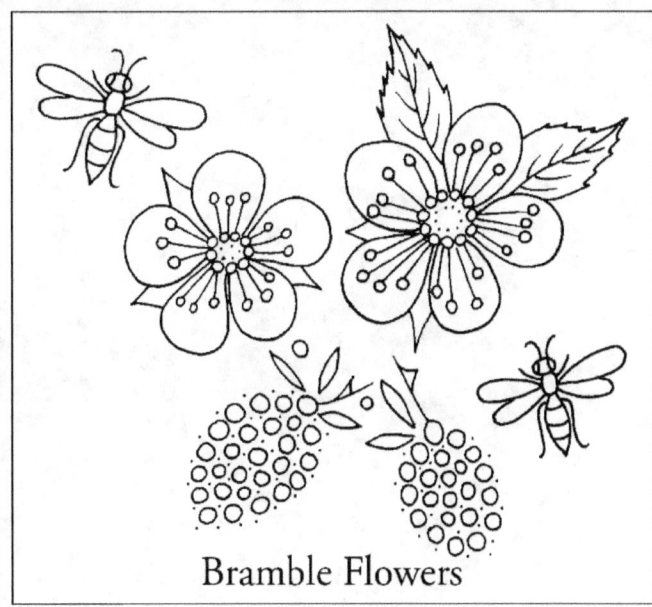

Bramble Flowers

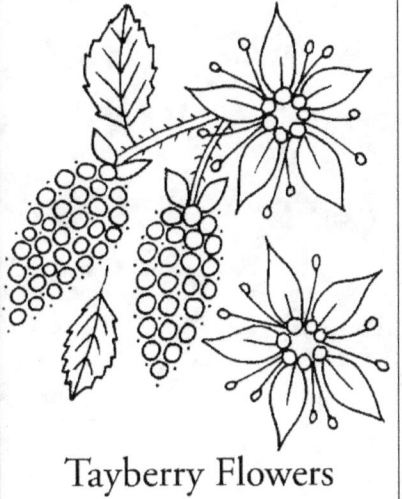

Tayberry Flowers

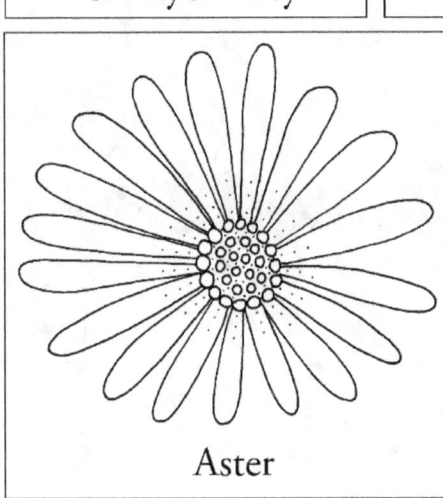

Aster

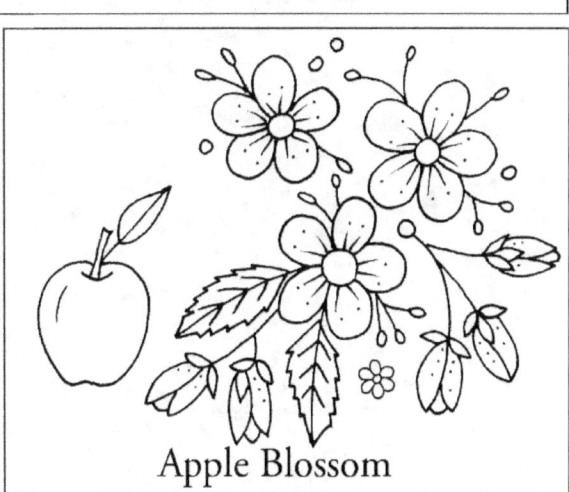

Apple Blossom

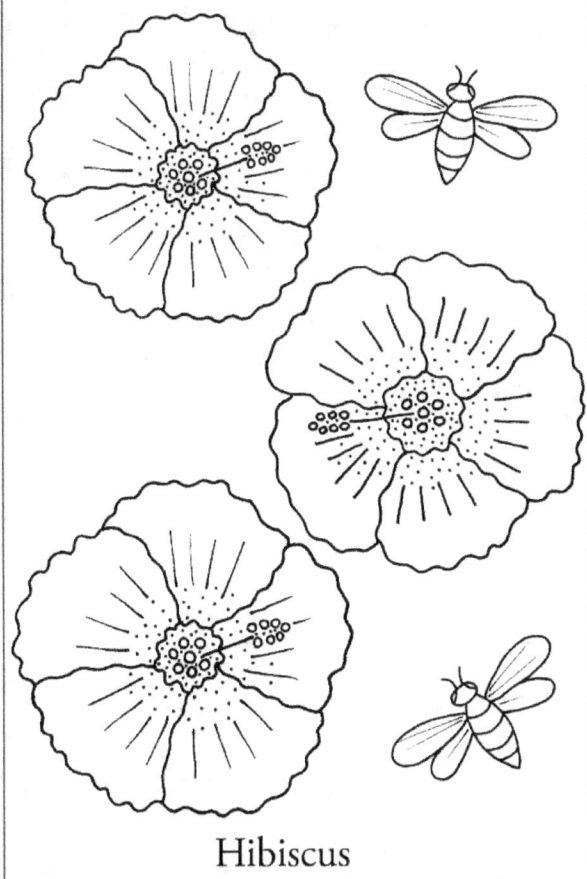

Hibiscus

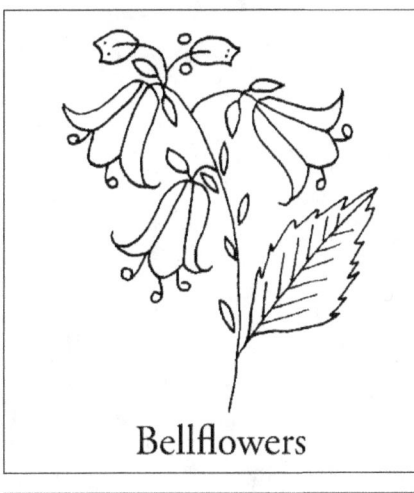

Bellflowers

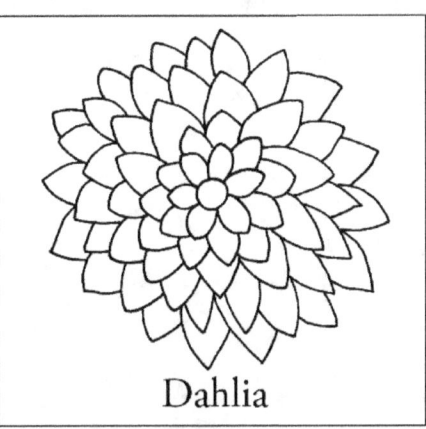

Dahlia

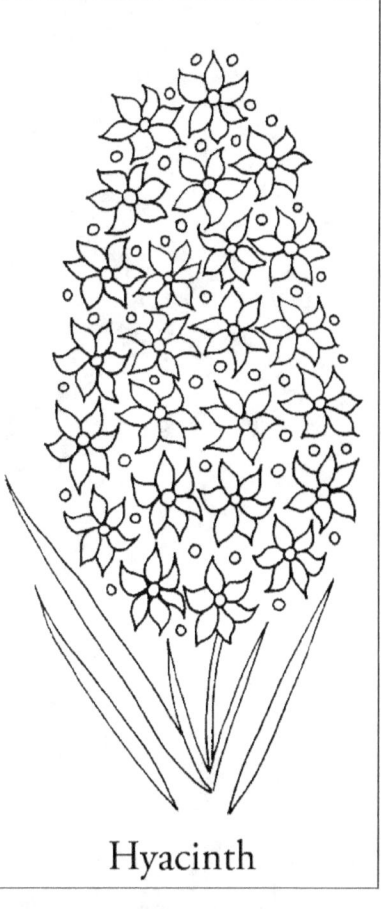

Hyacinth

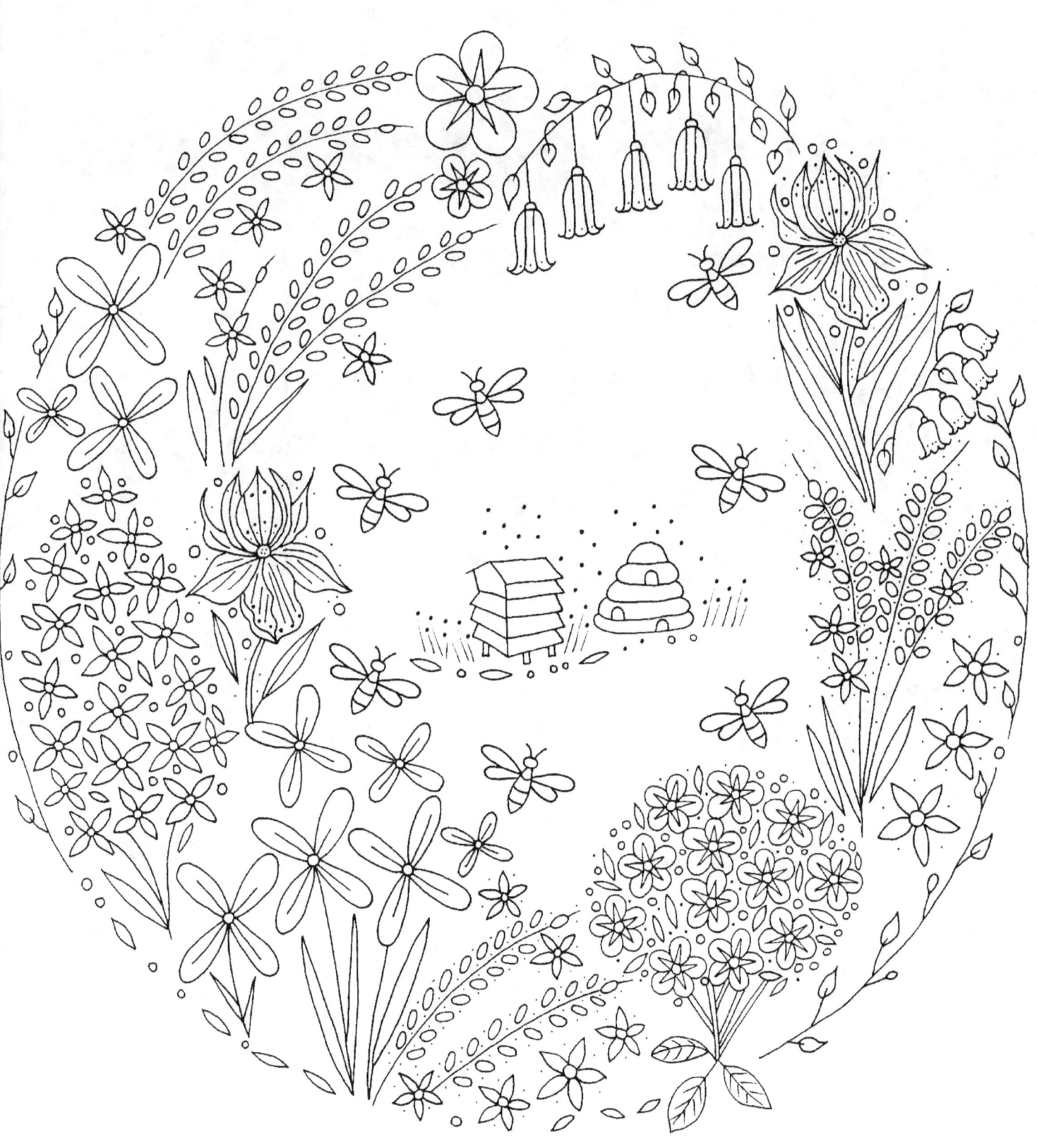

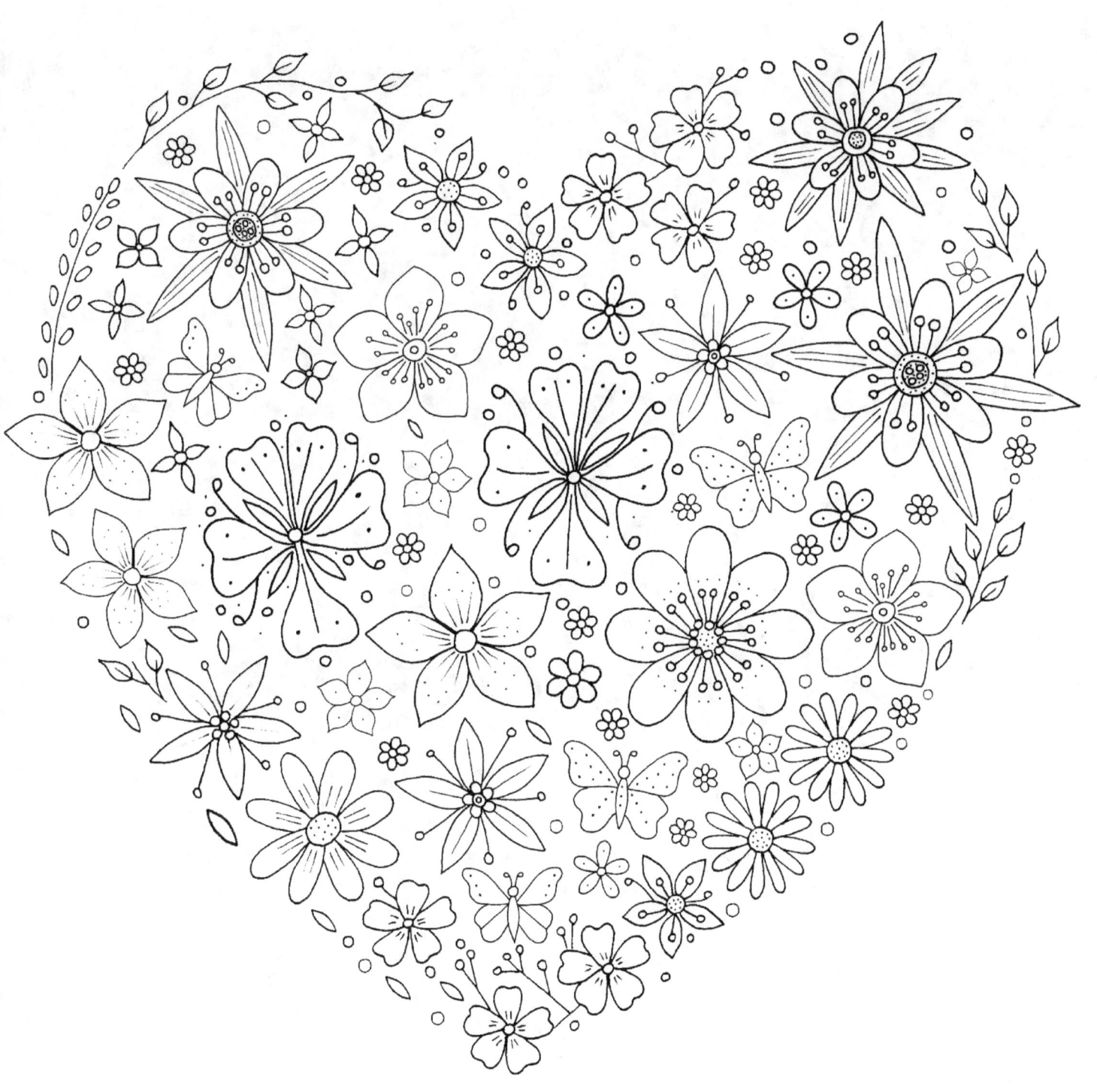

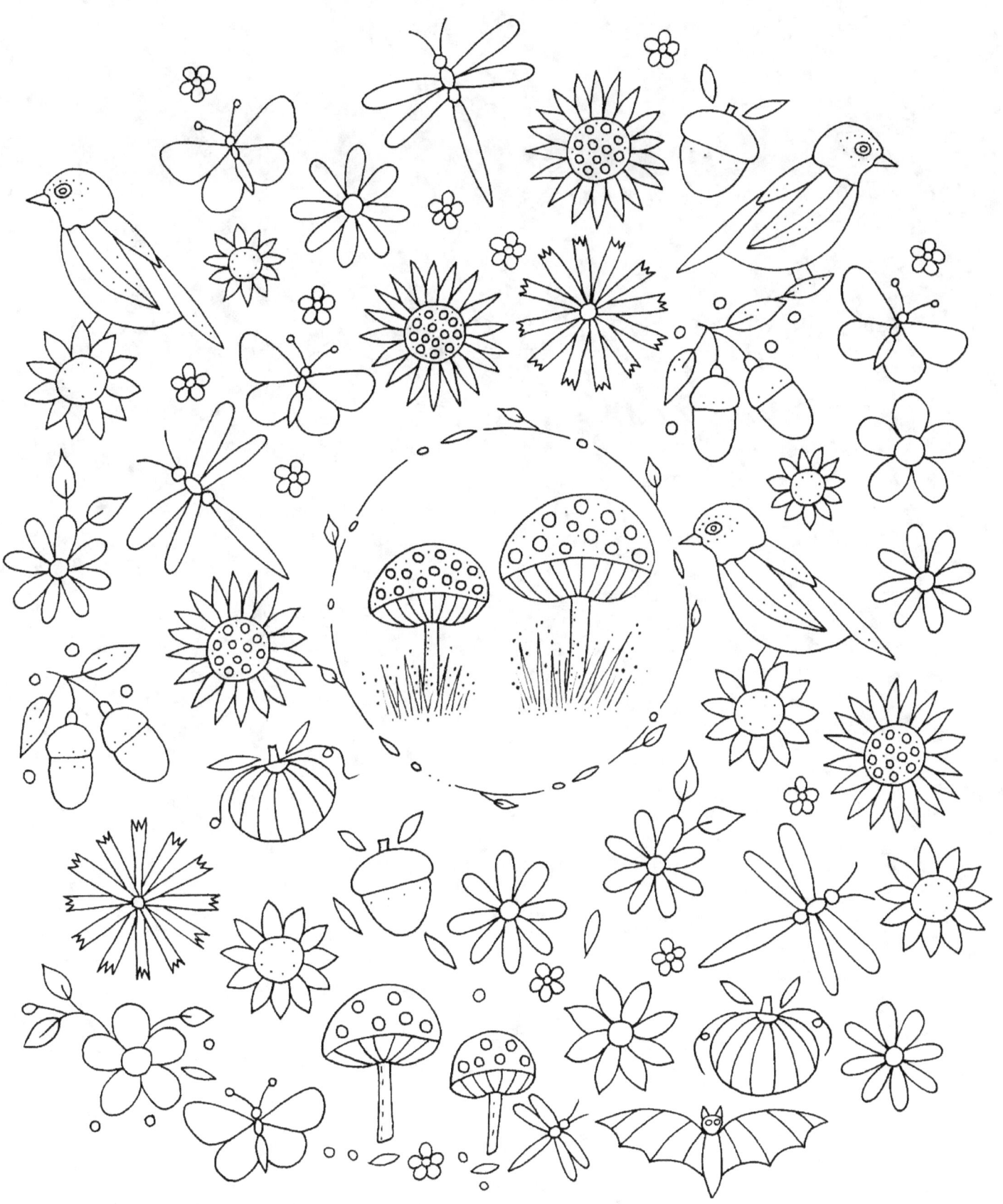

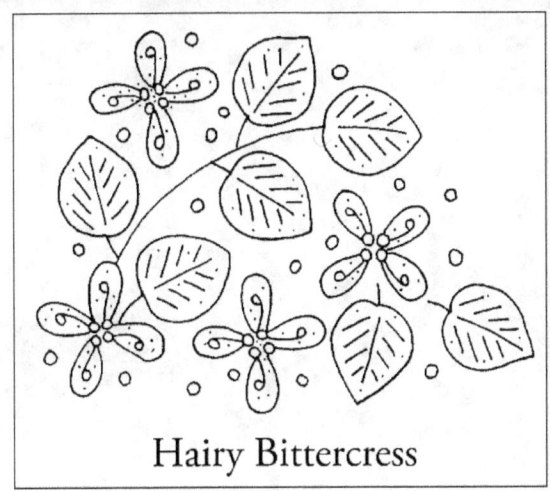

Hairy Bittercress

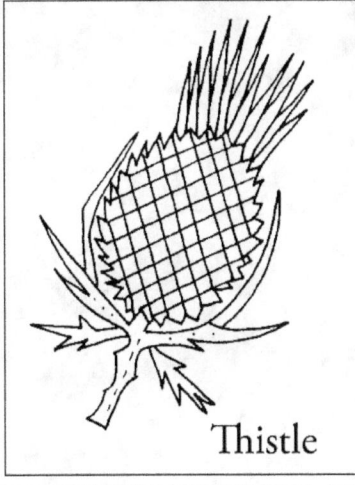

Thistle

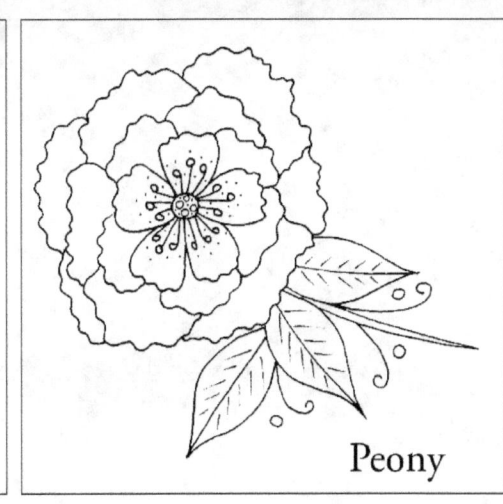

Peony

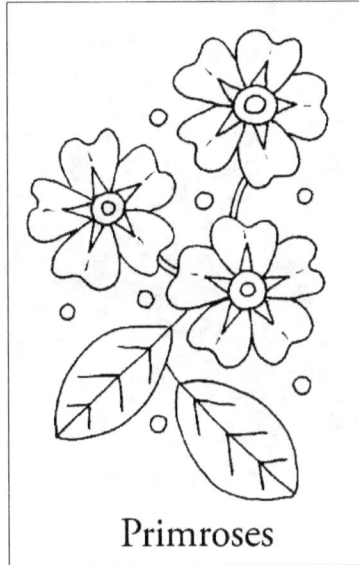

Primroses

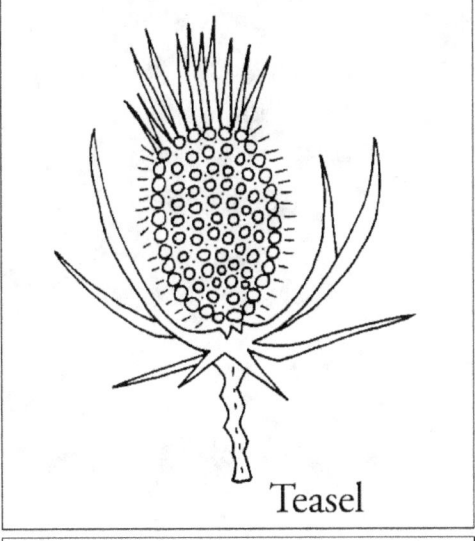

Teasel

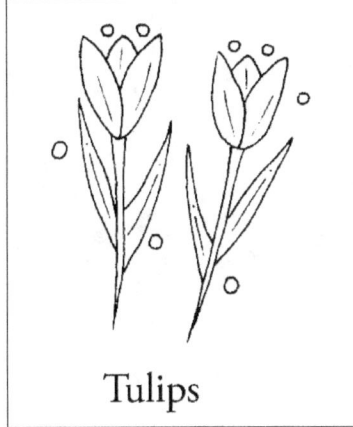

Tulips

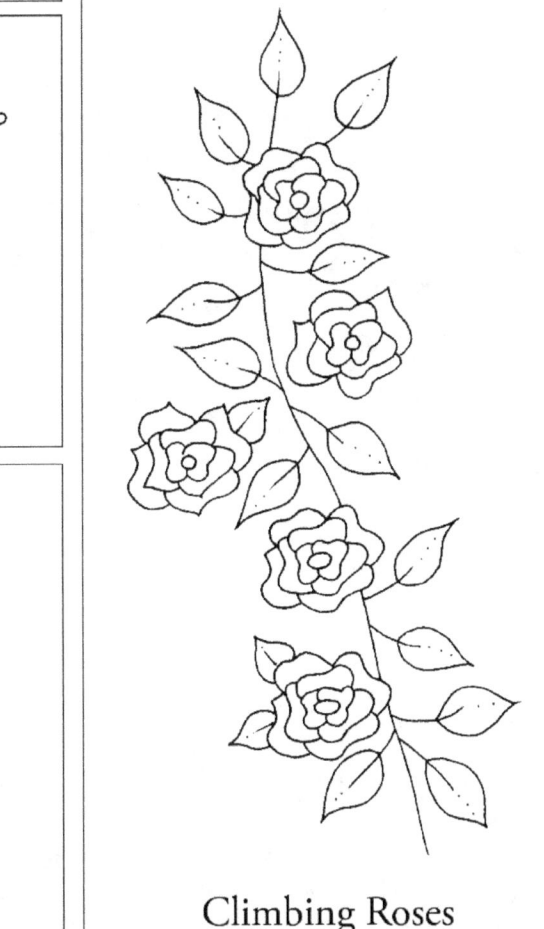

Climbing Roses

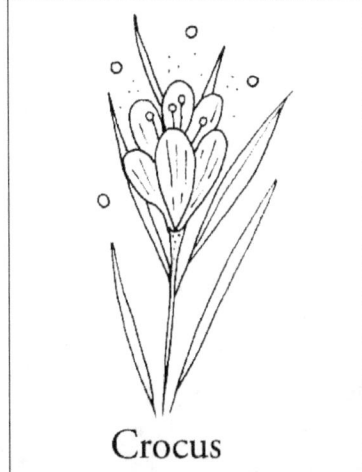

Crocus

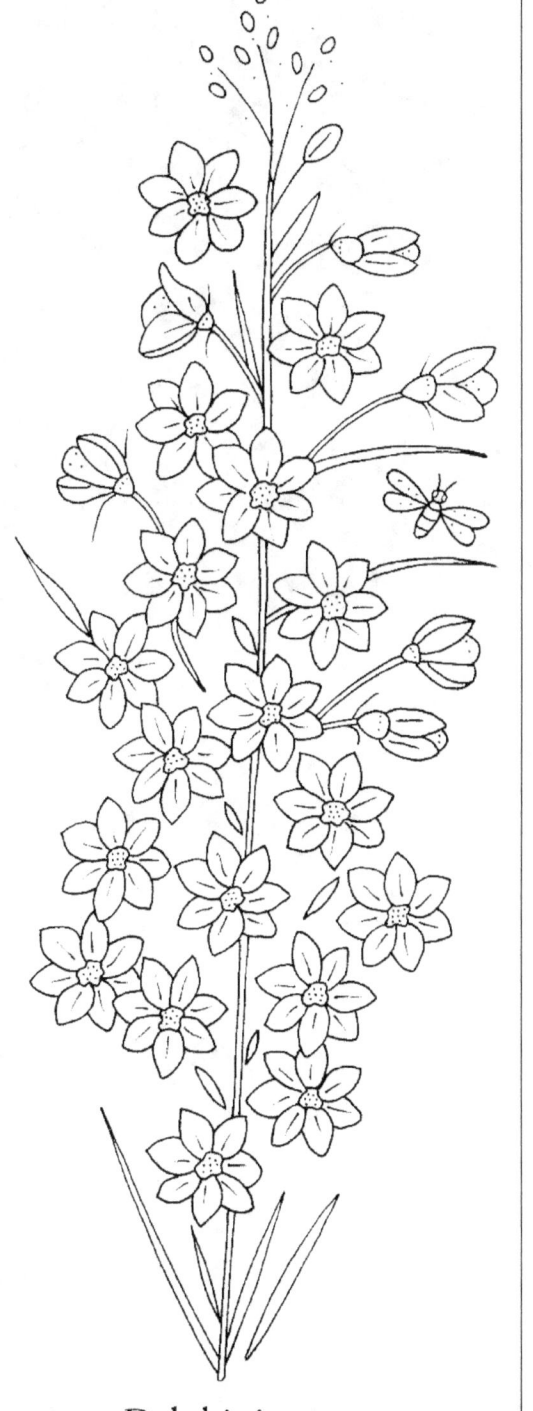

Delphiniums

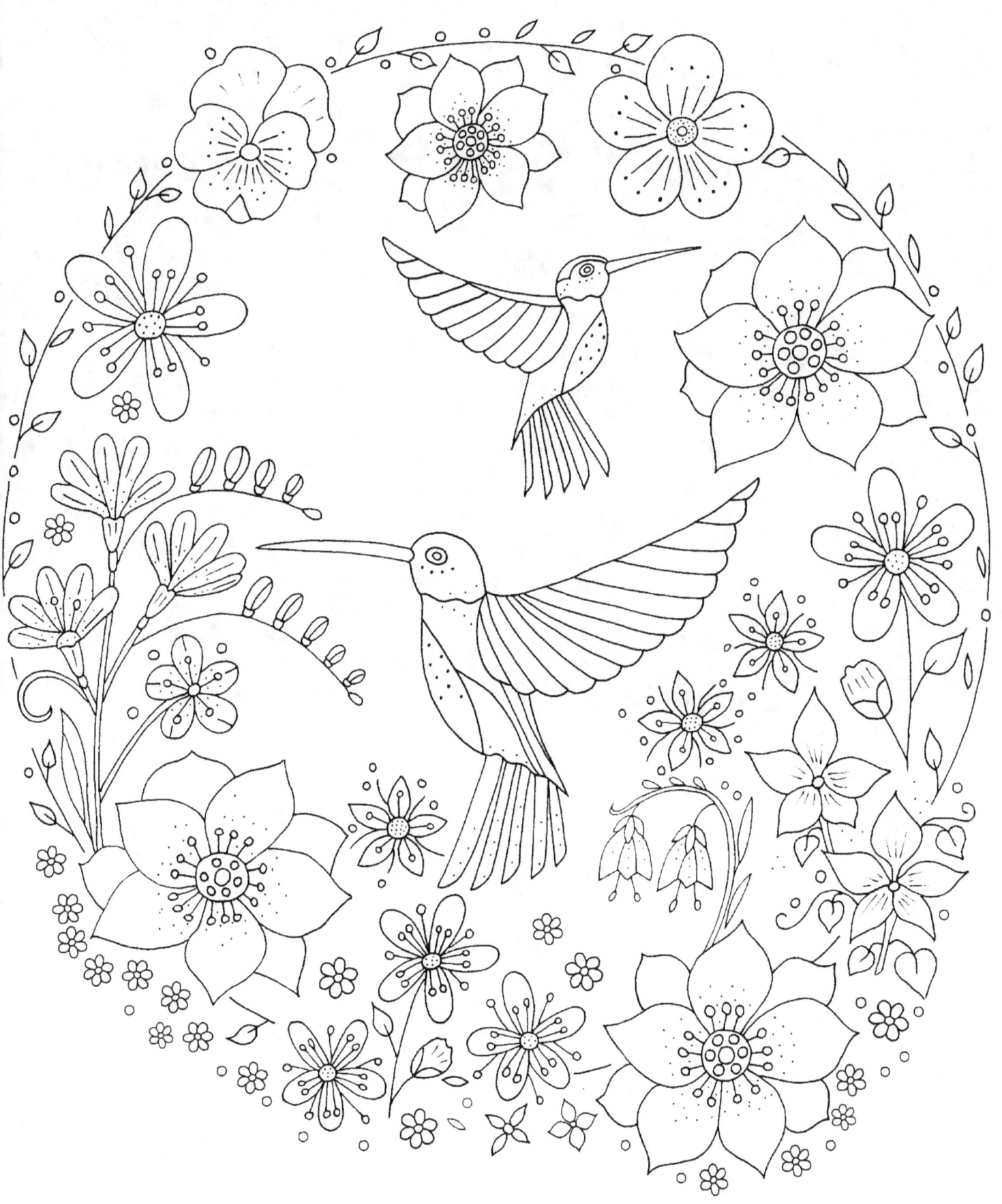

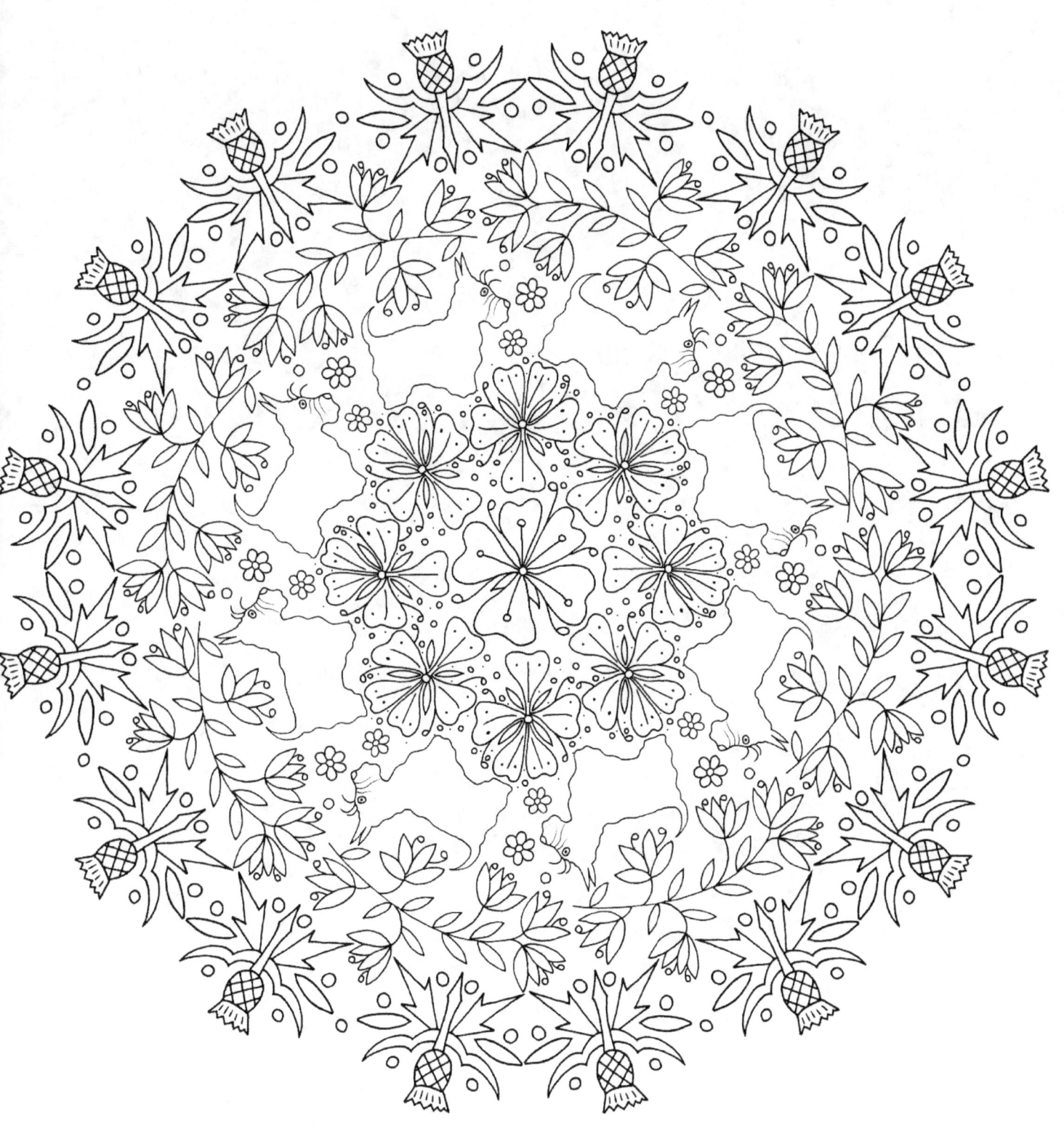

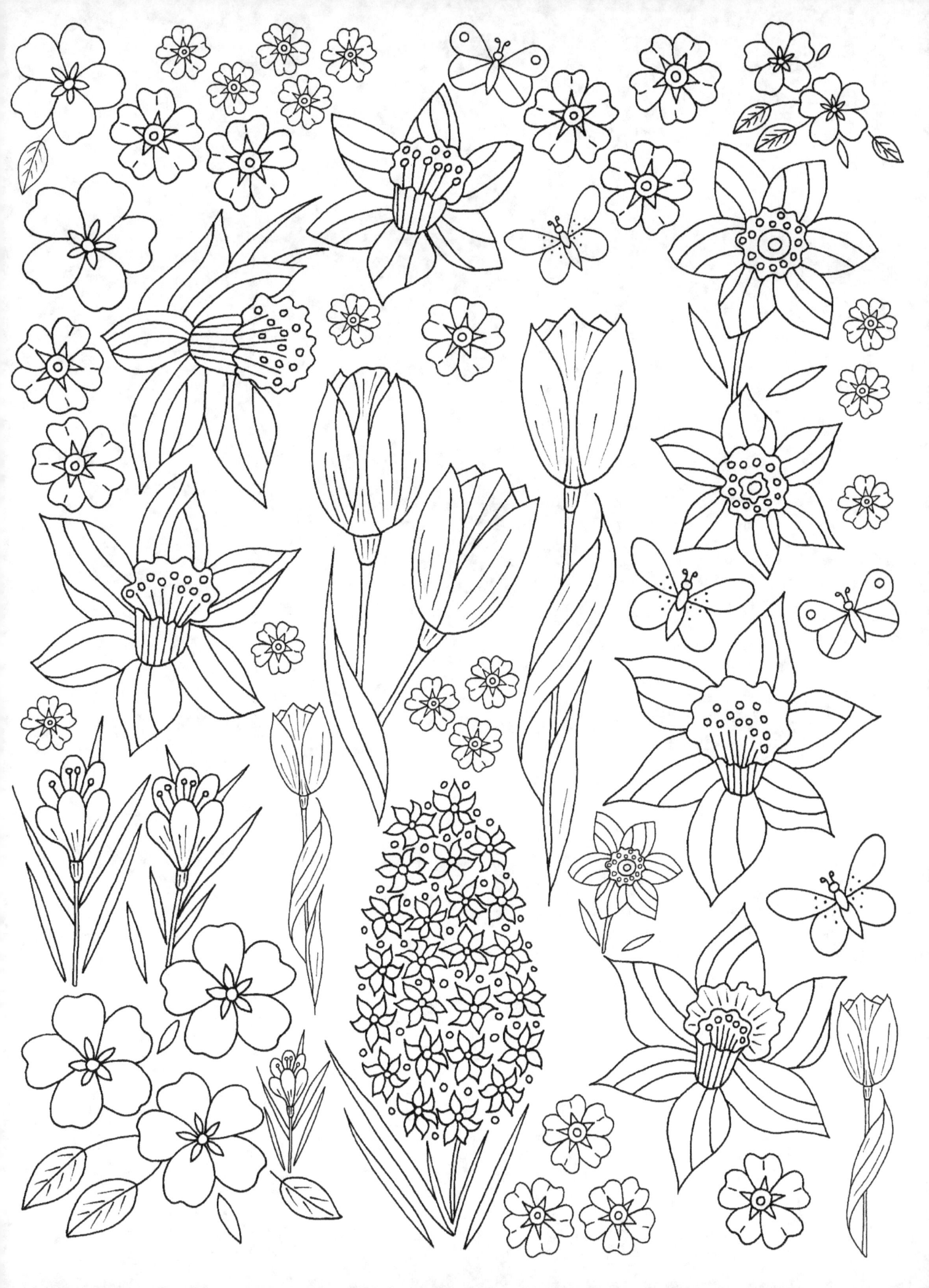

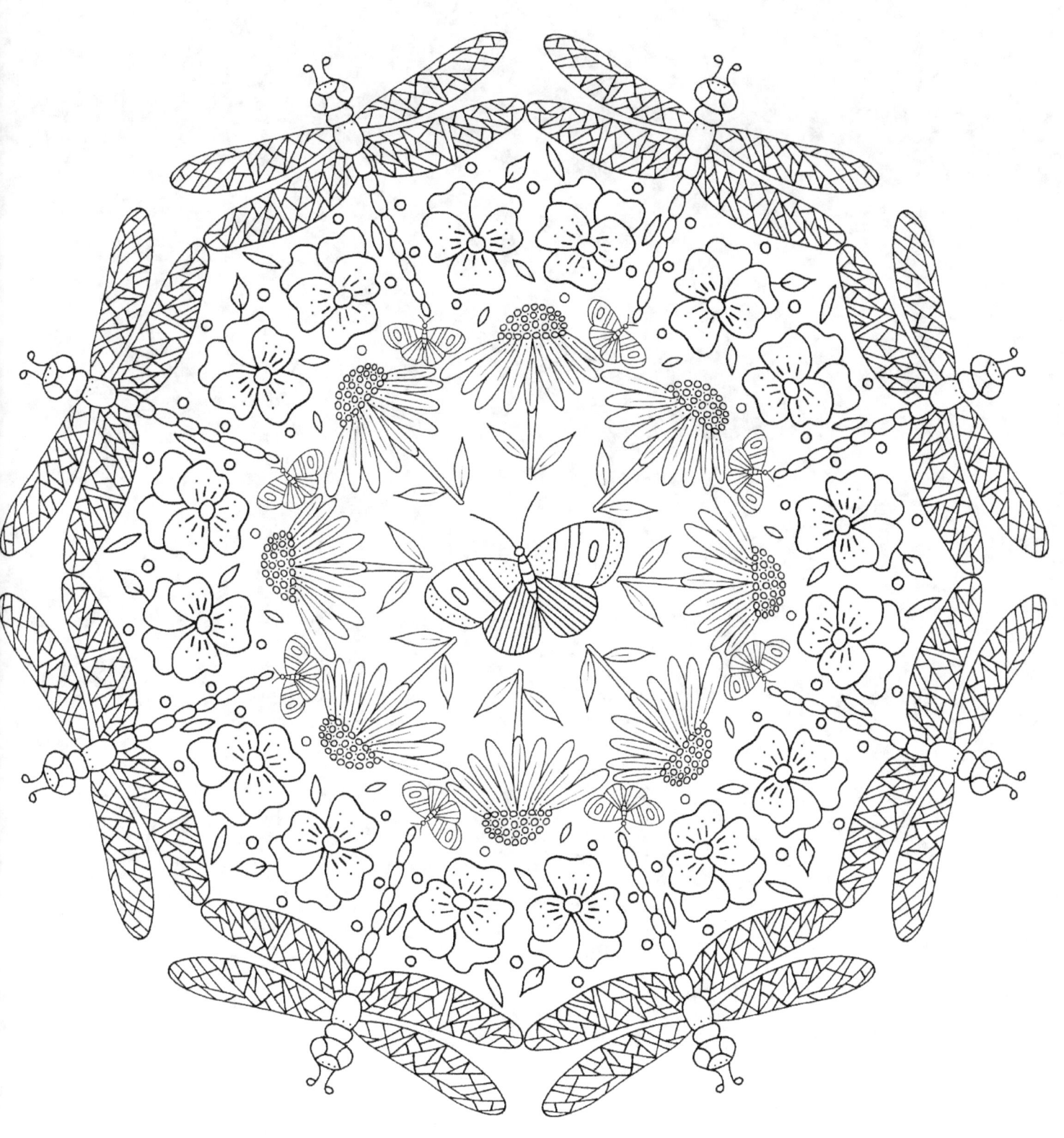

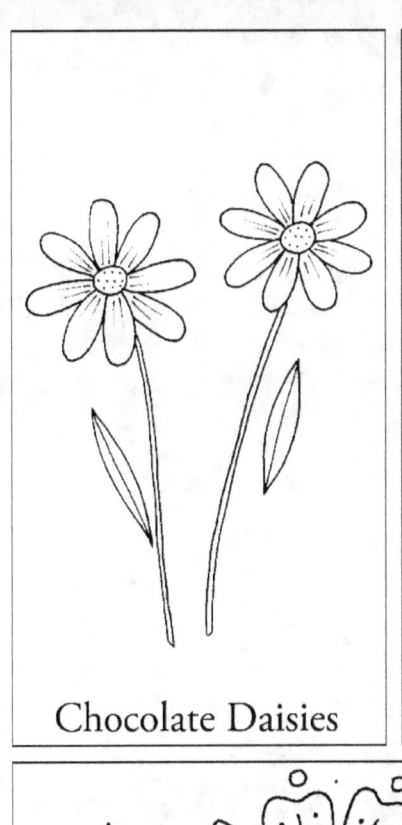

Chocolate Daisies

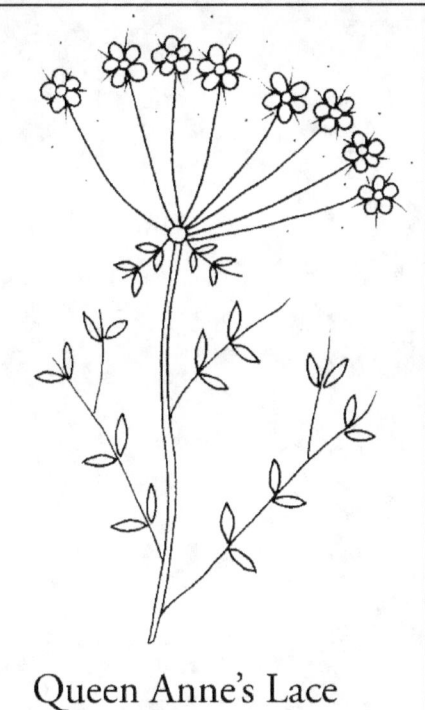

Queen Anne's Lace

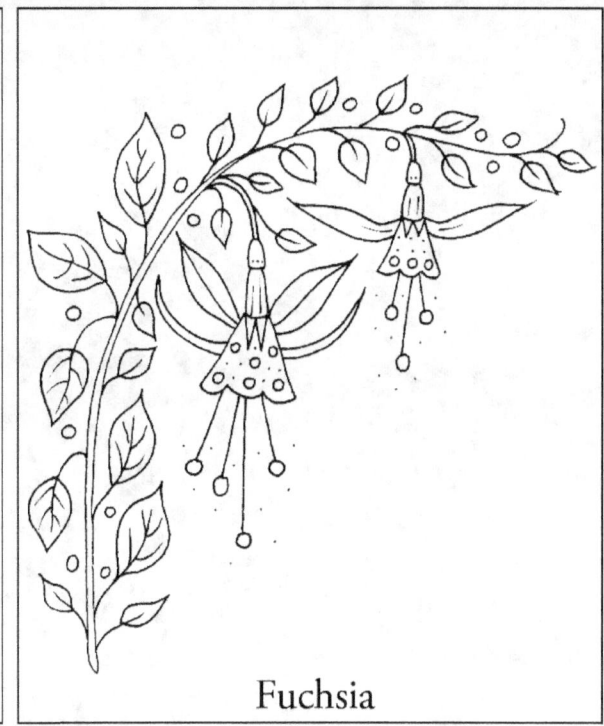

Fuchsia

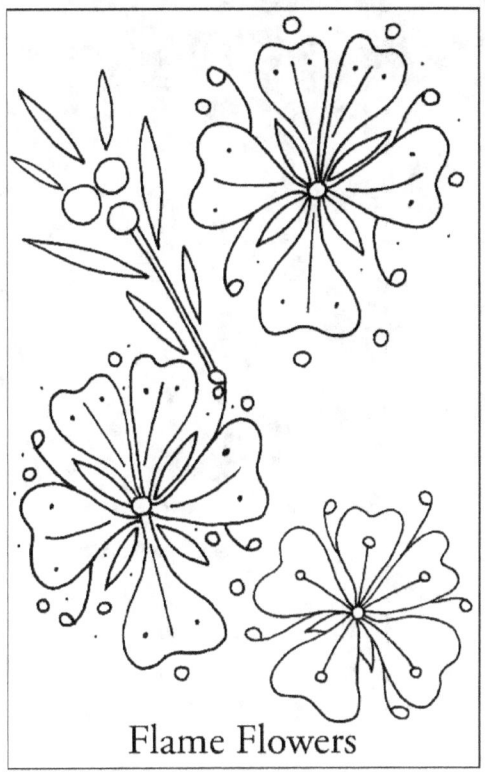

Flame Flowers

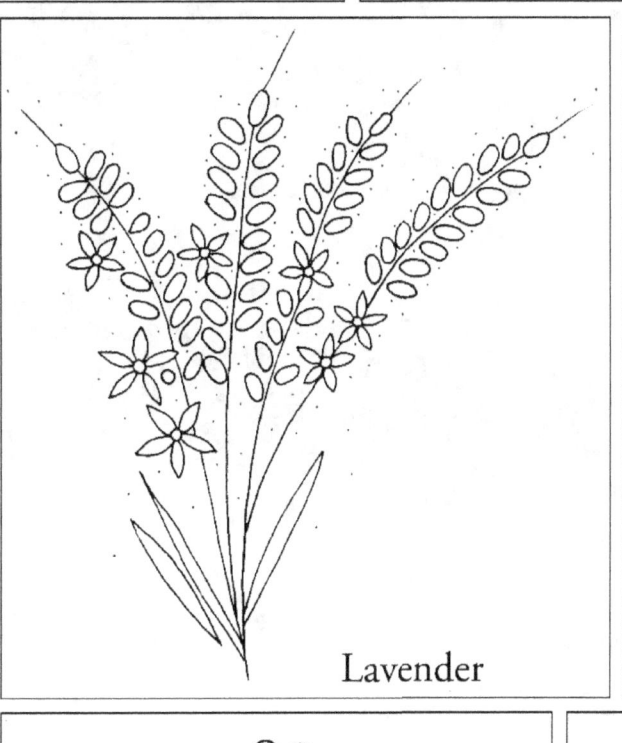

Lavender

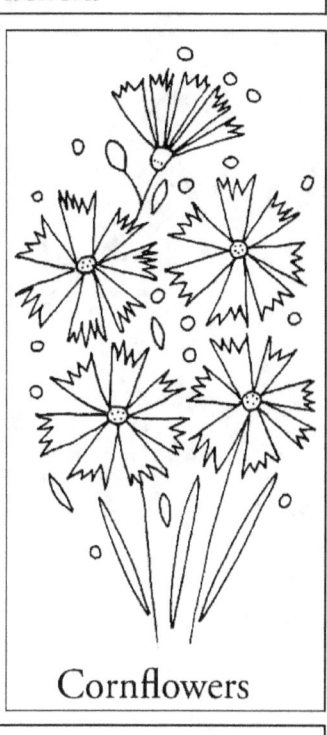

Cornflowers

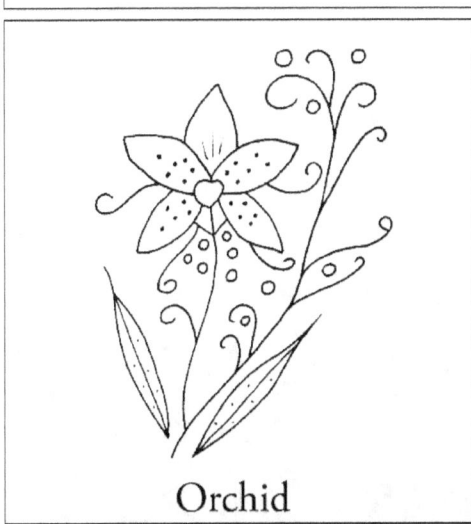

Orchid

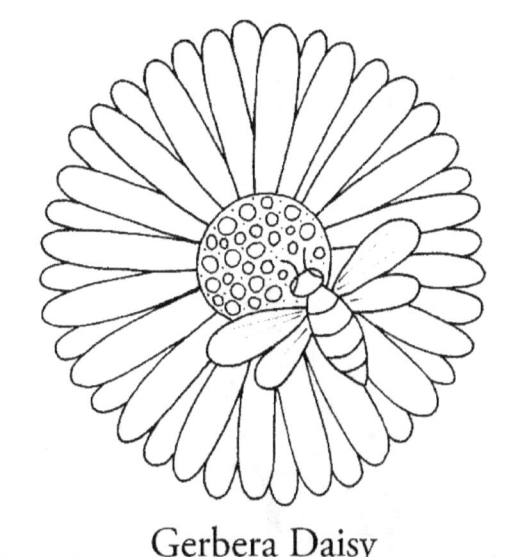

Gerbera Daisy

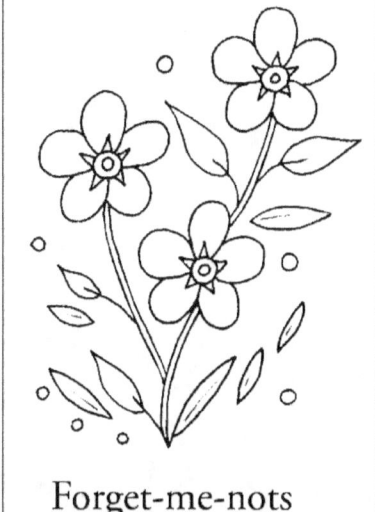

Forget-me-nots

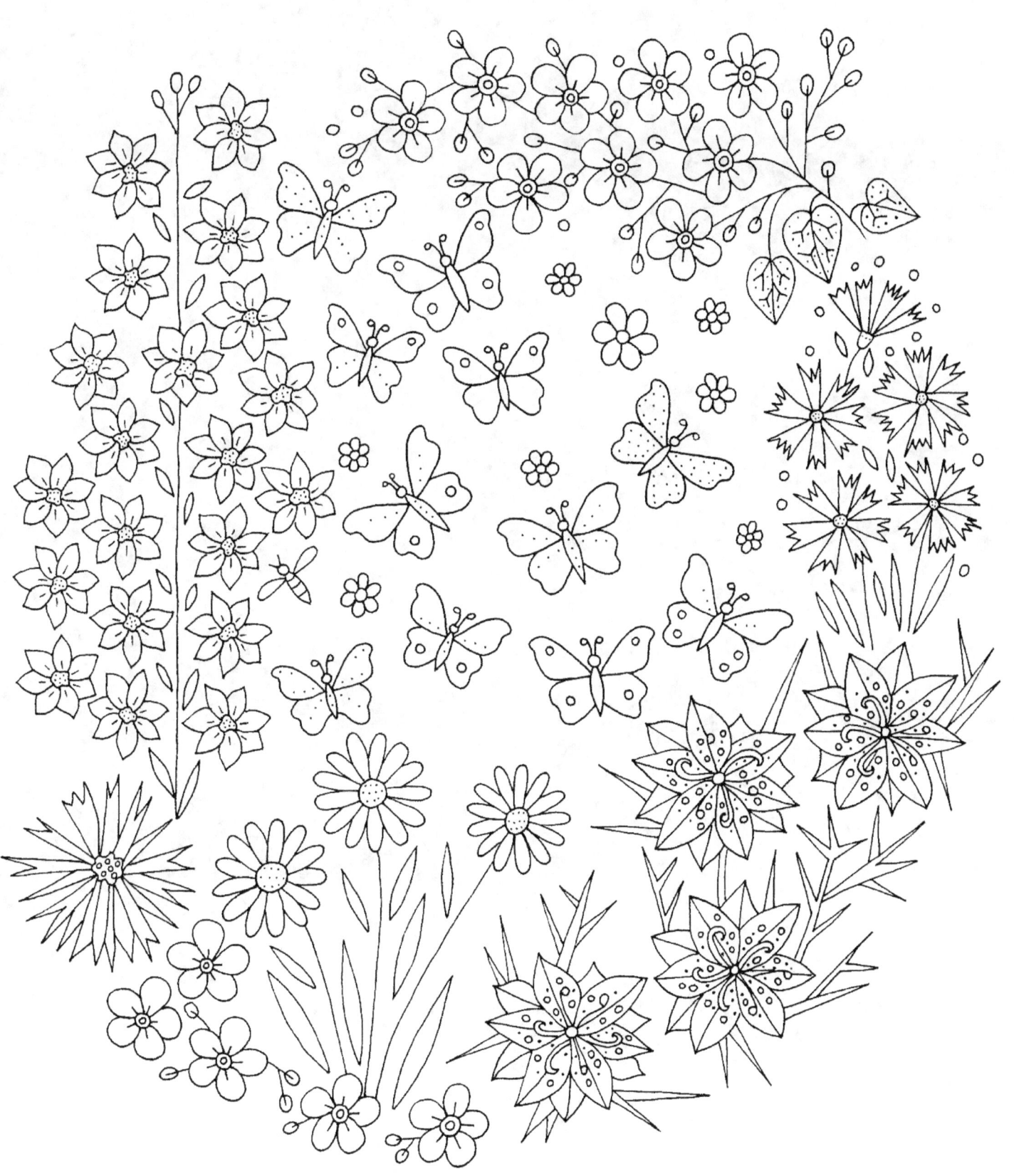

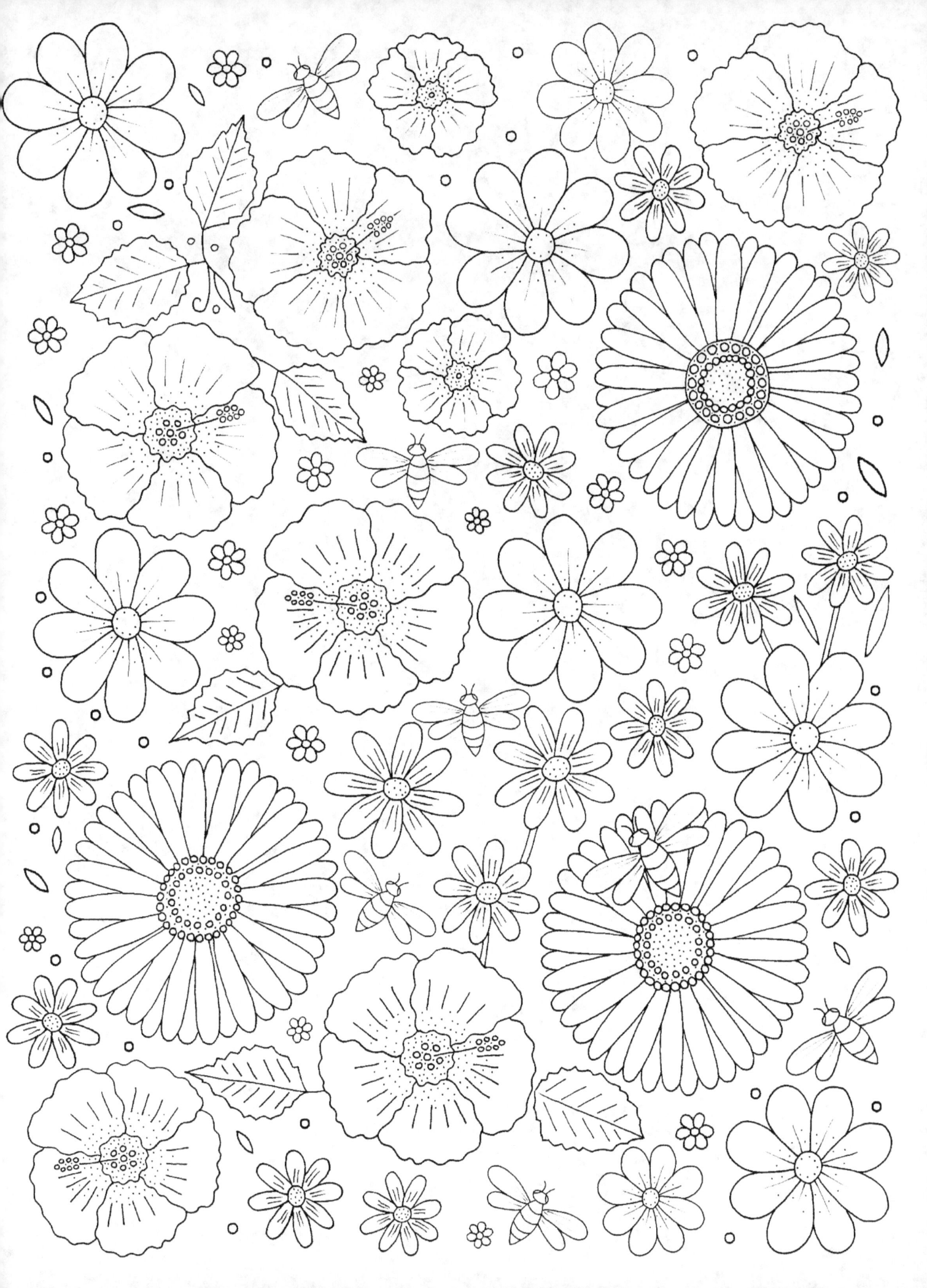

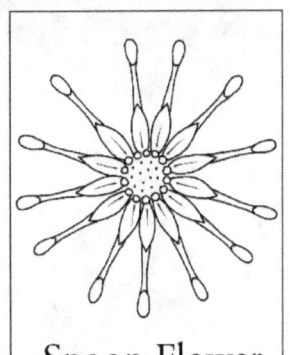

Spoon Flower

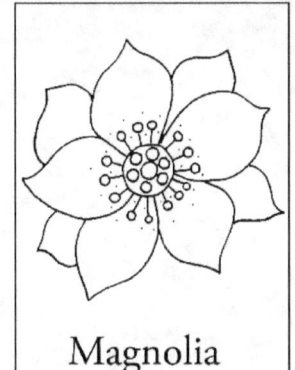

Magnolia

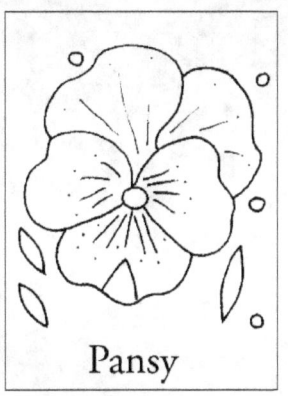

Pansy

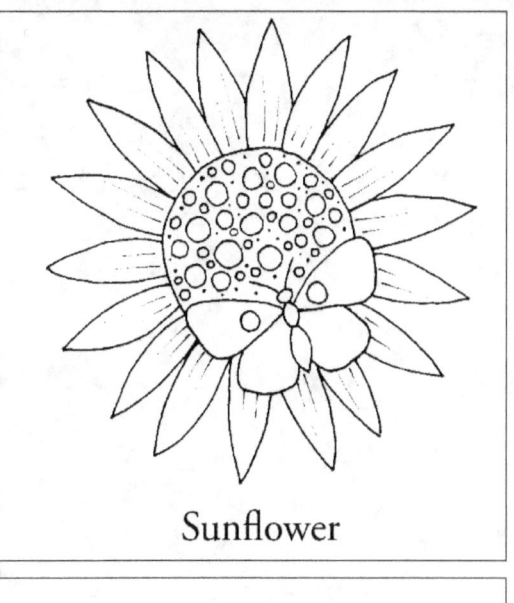

Sunflower

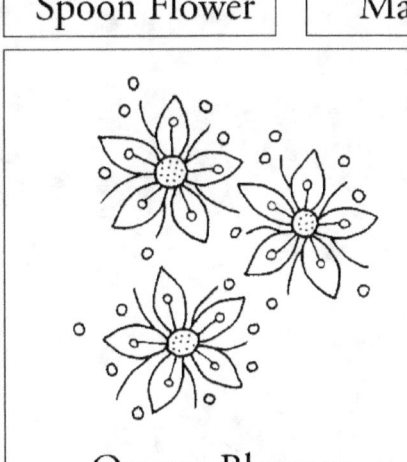

Orange Blossom

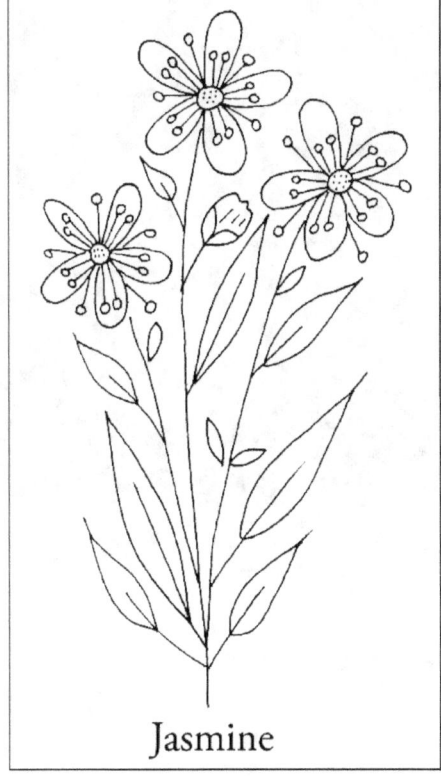

Jasmine

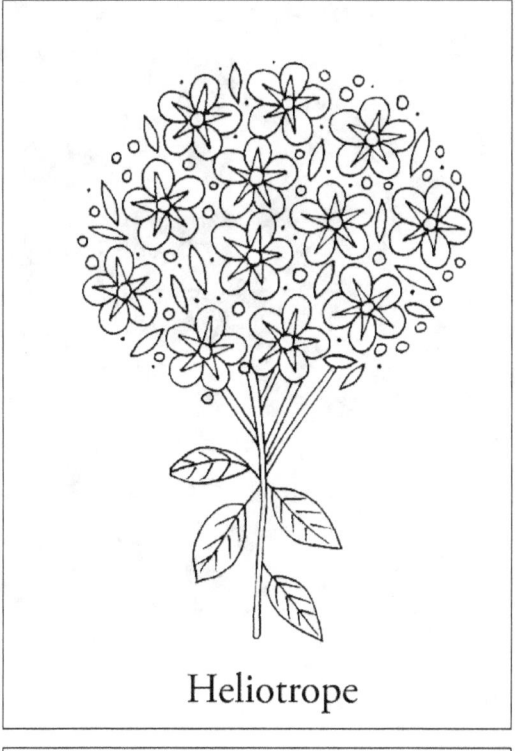

Heliotrope

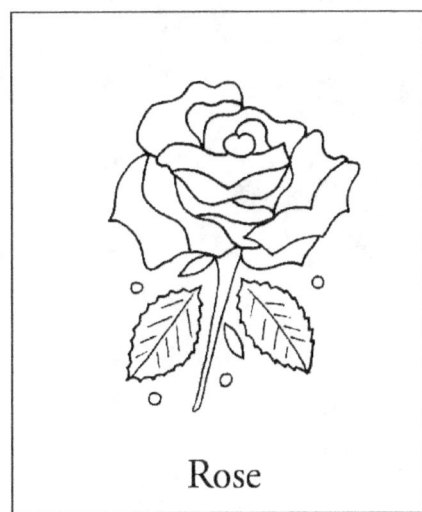

Rose

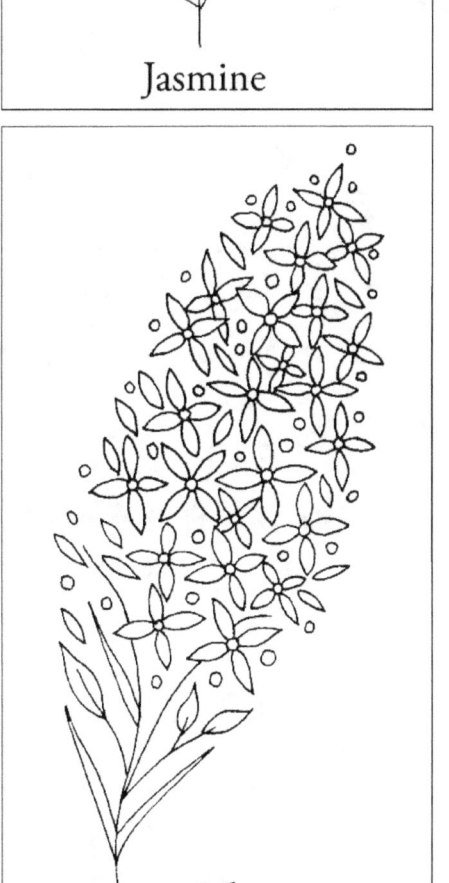

Lilac

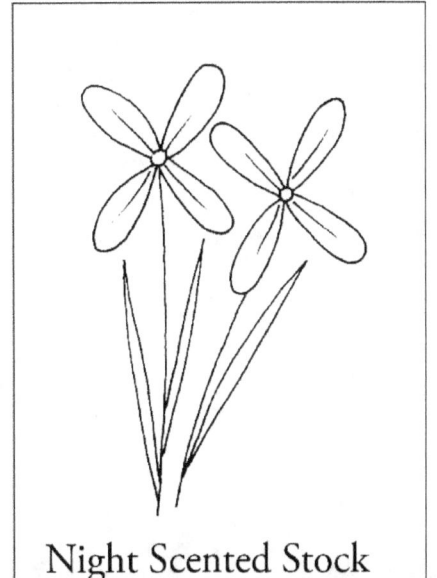

Night Scented Stock

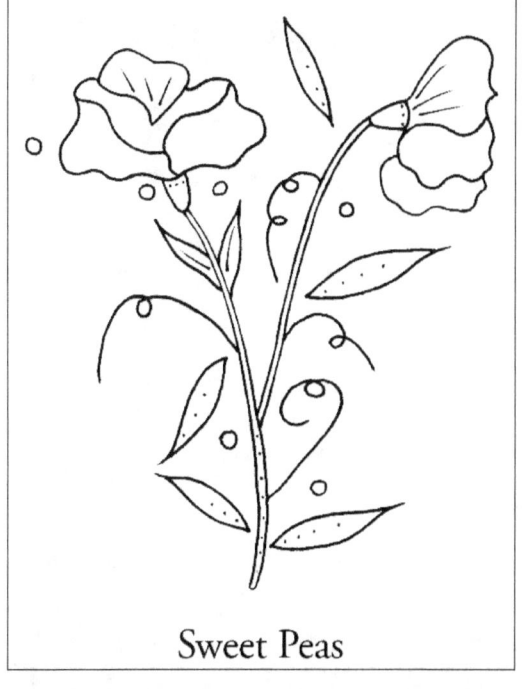

Sweet Peas

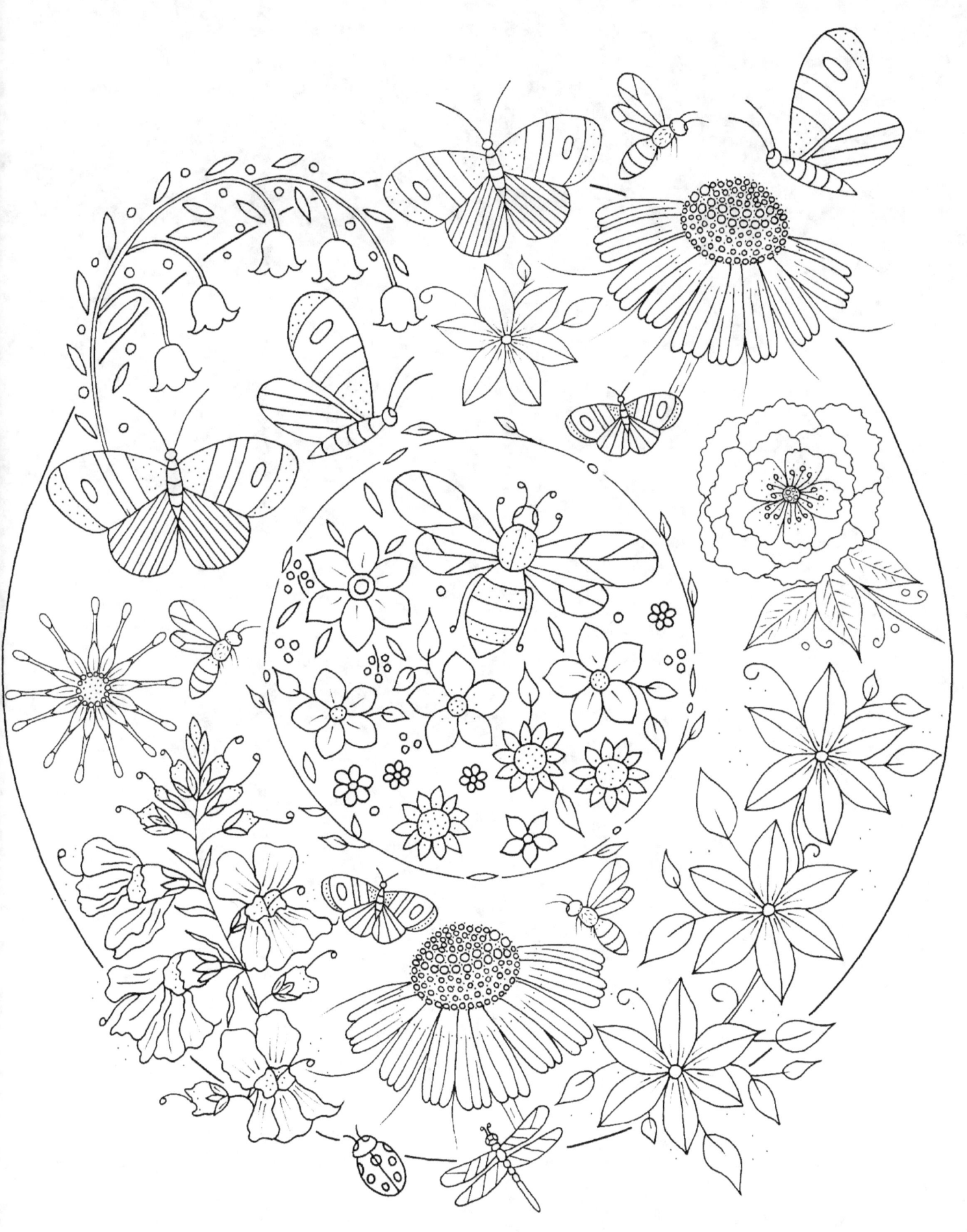

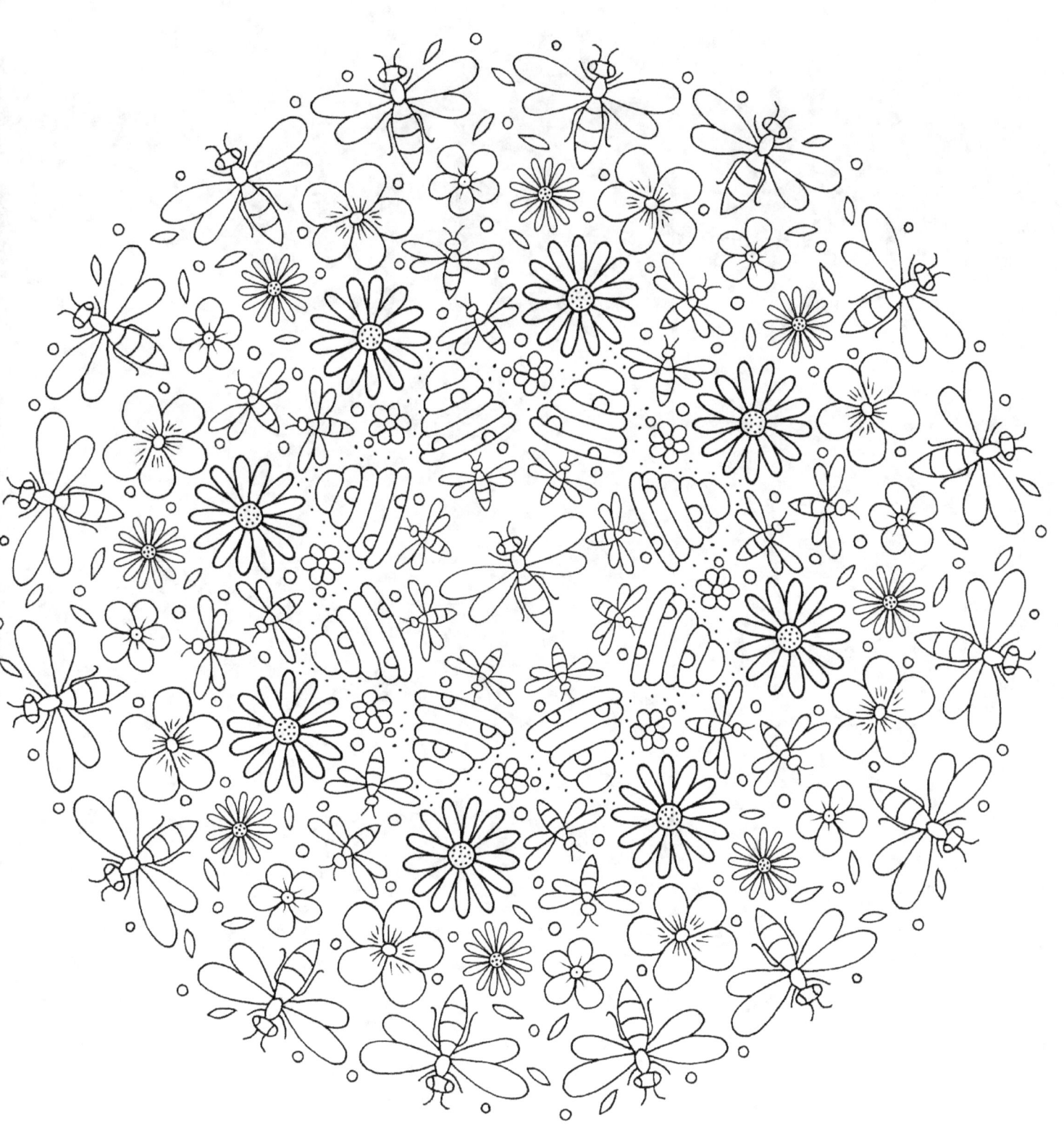

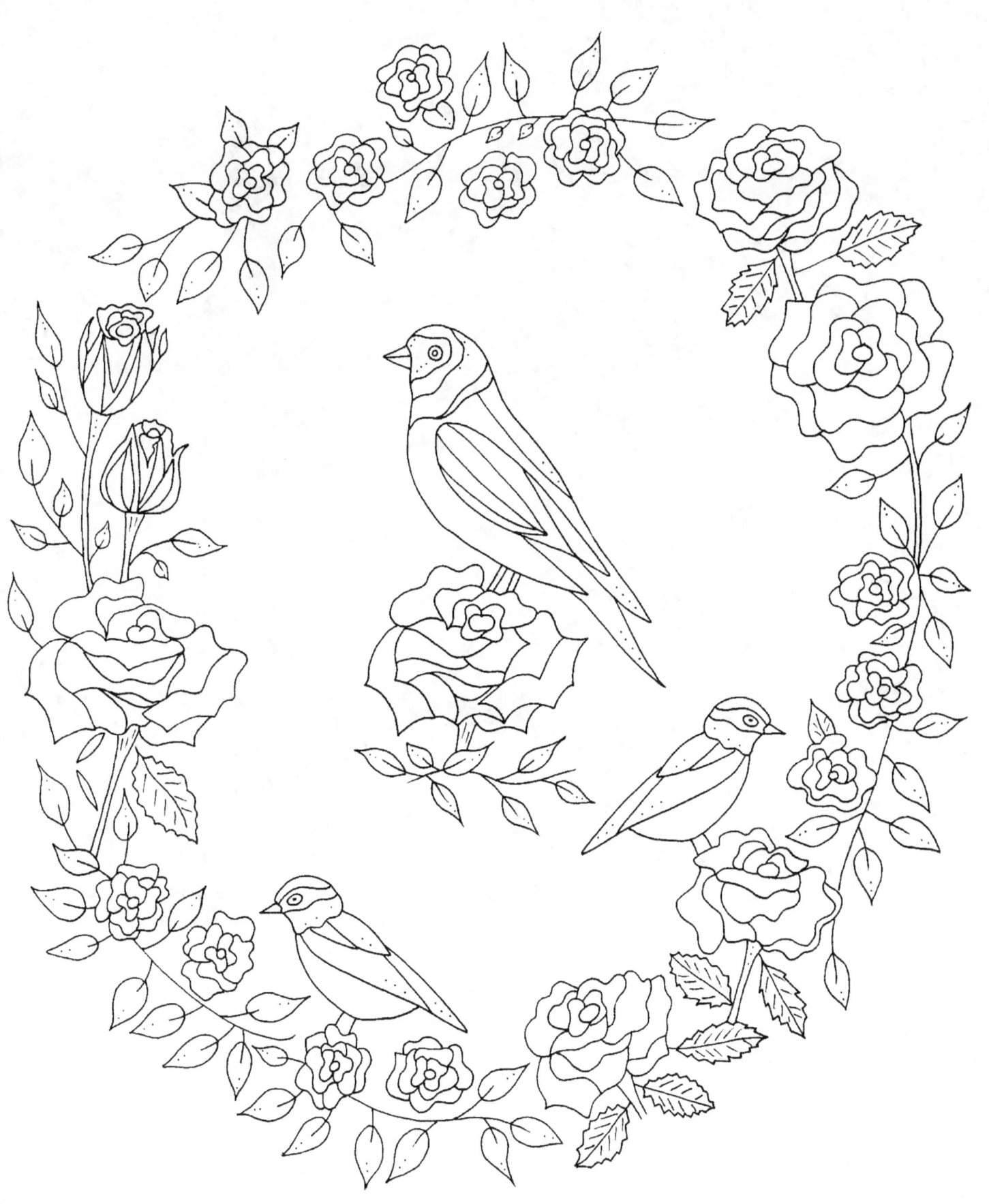

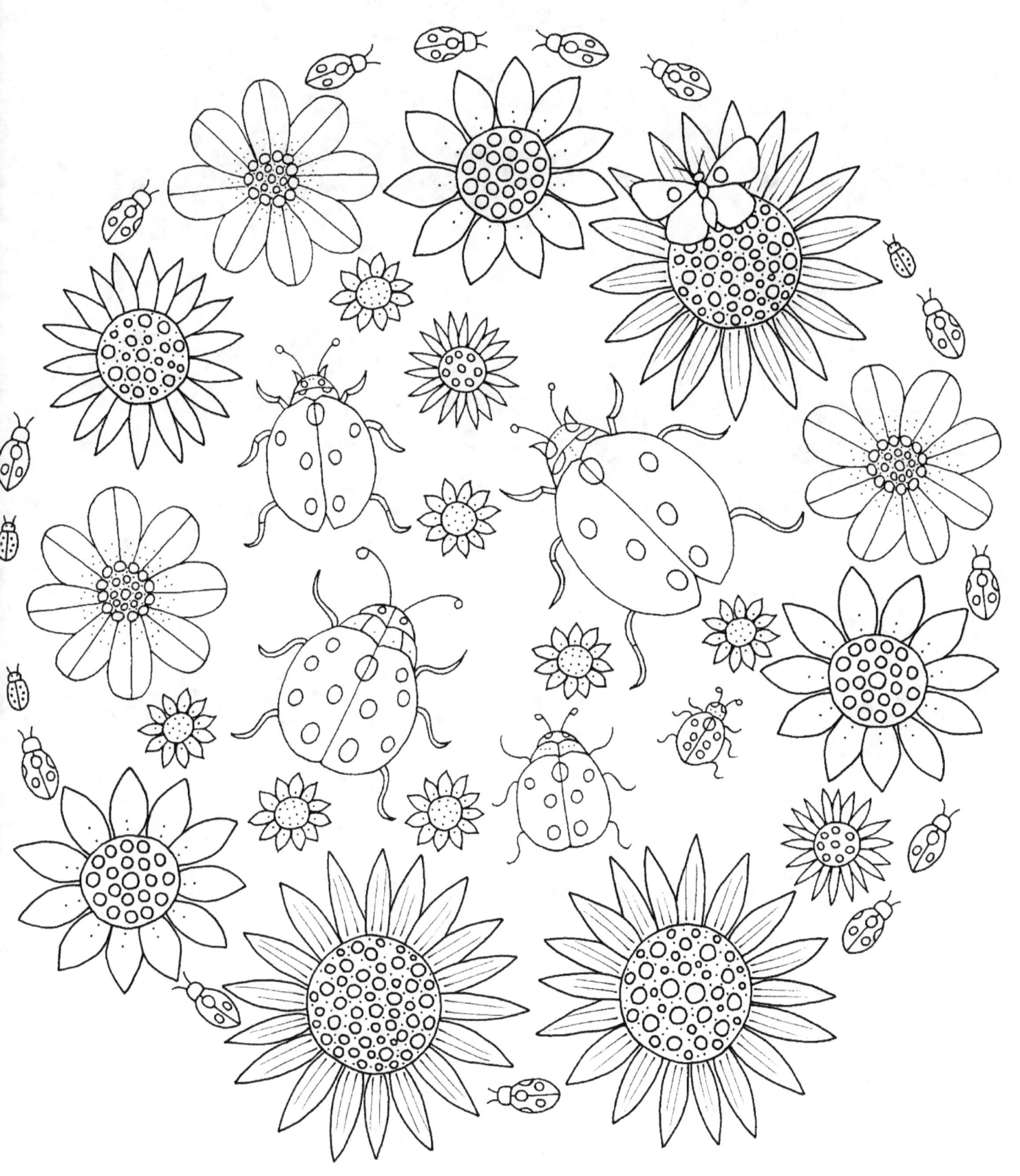

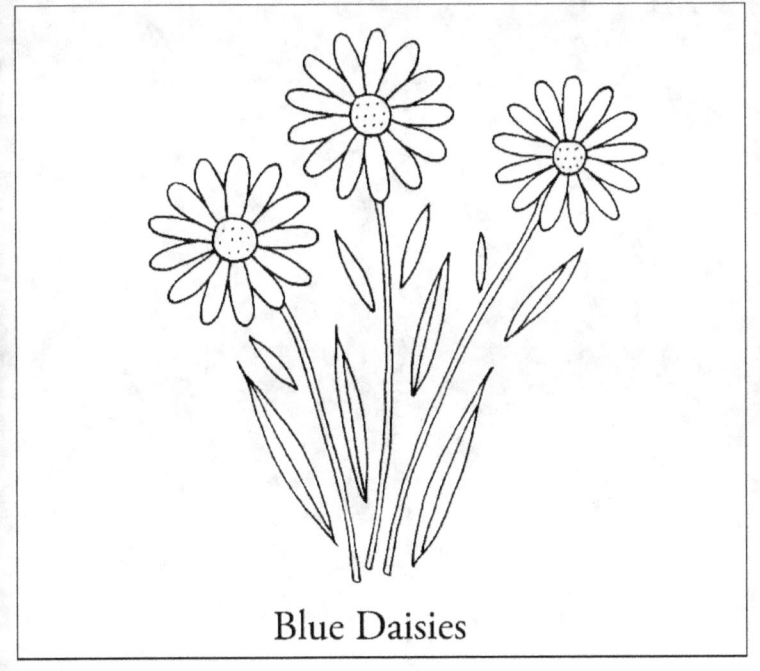

Blue Daisies

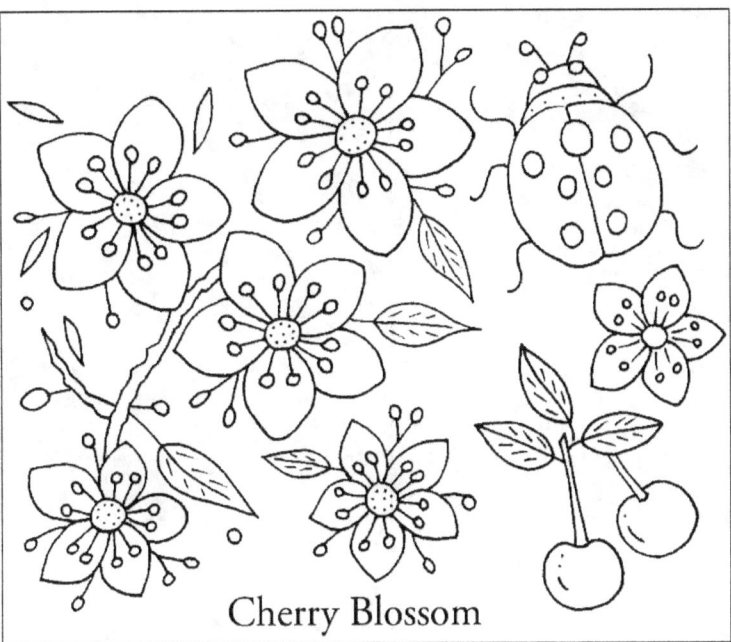

Cherry Blossom

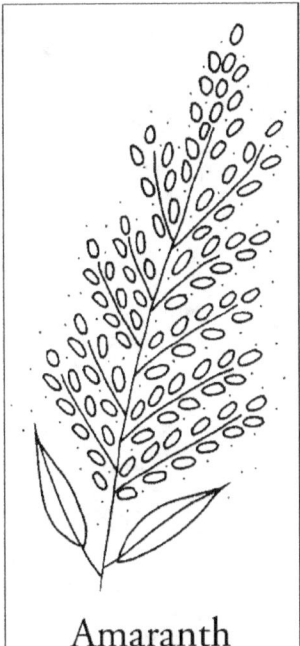

Amaranth

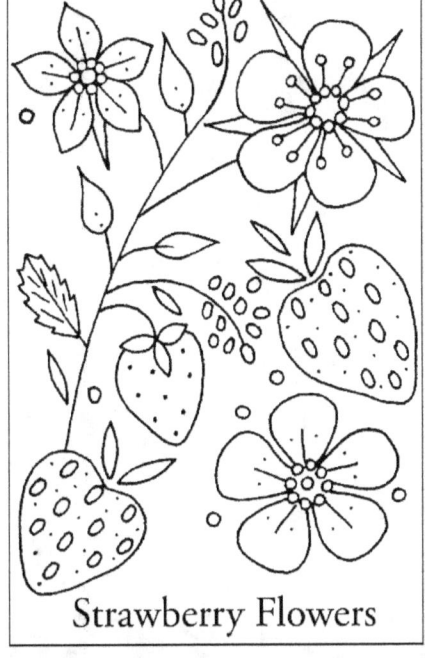

Strawberry Flowers

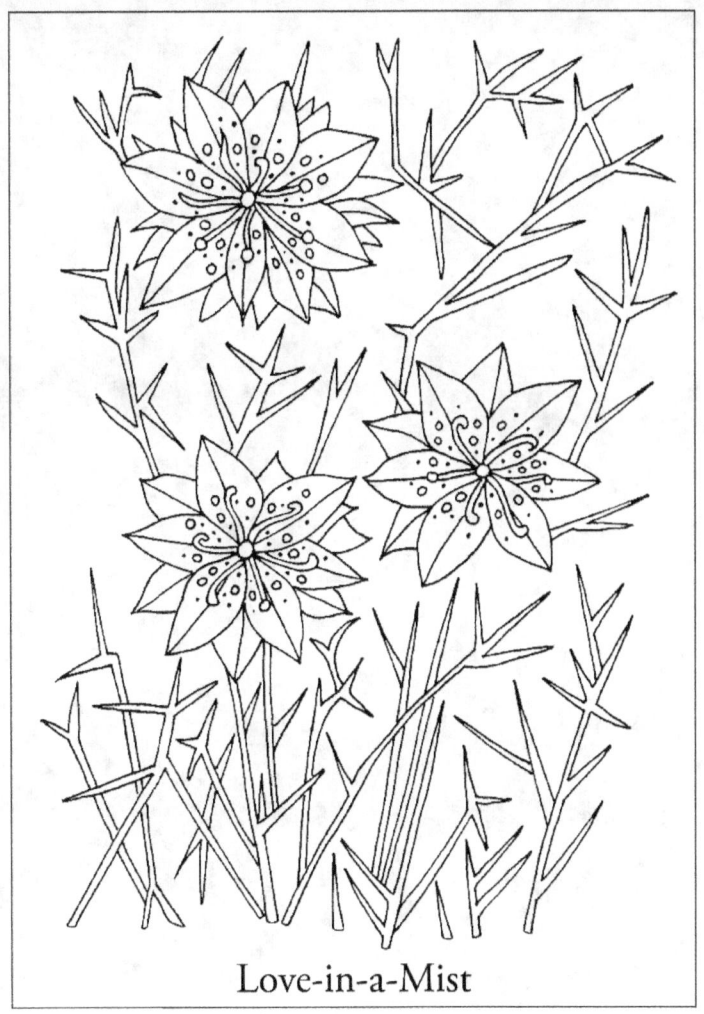

Love-in-a-Mist

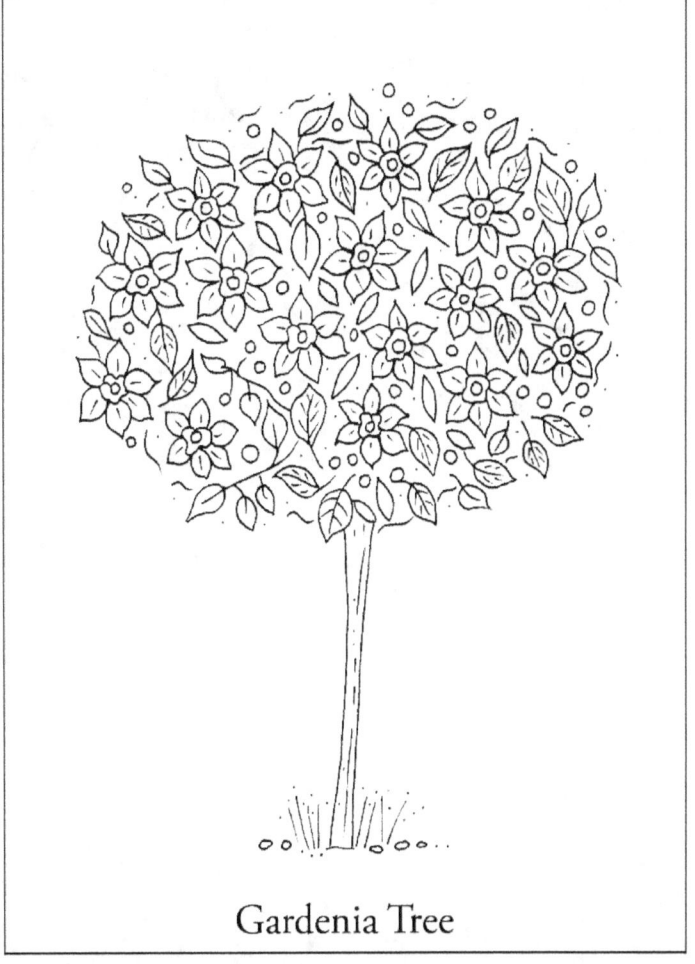

Gardenia Tree

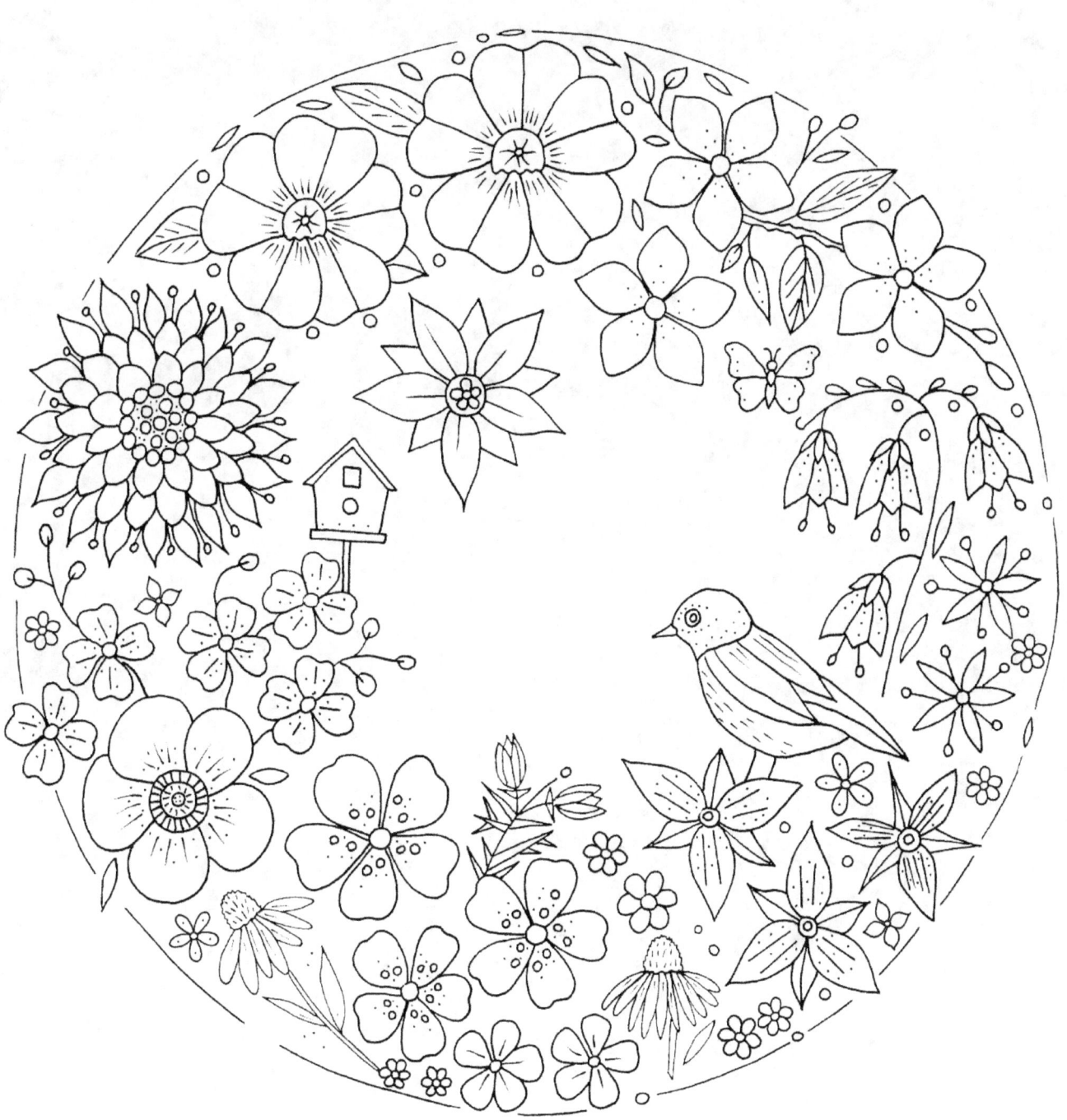

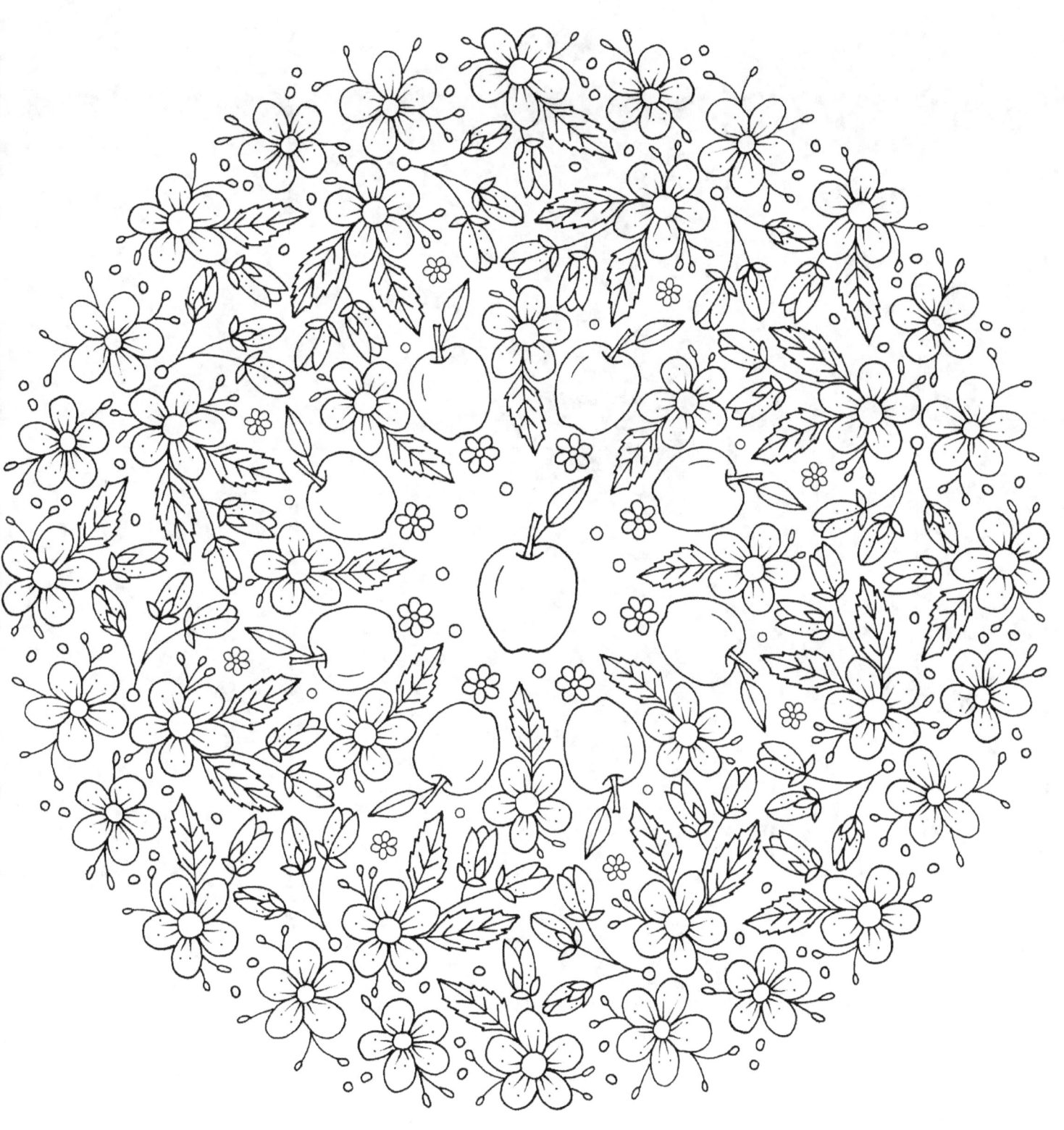

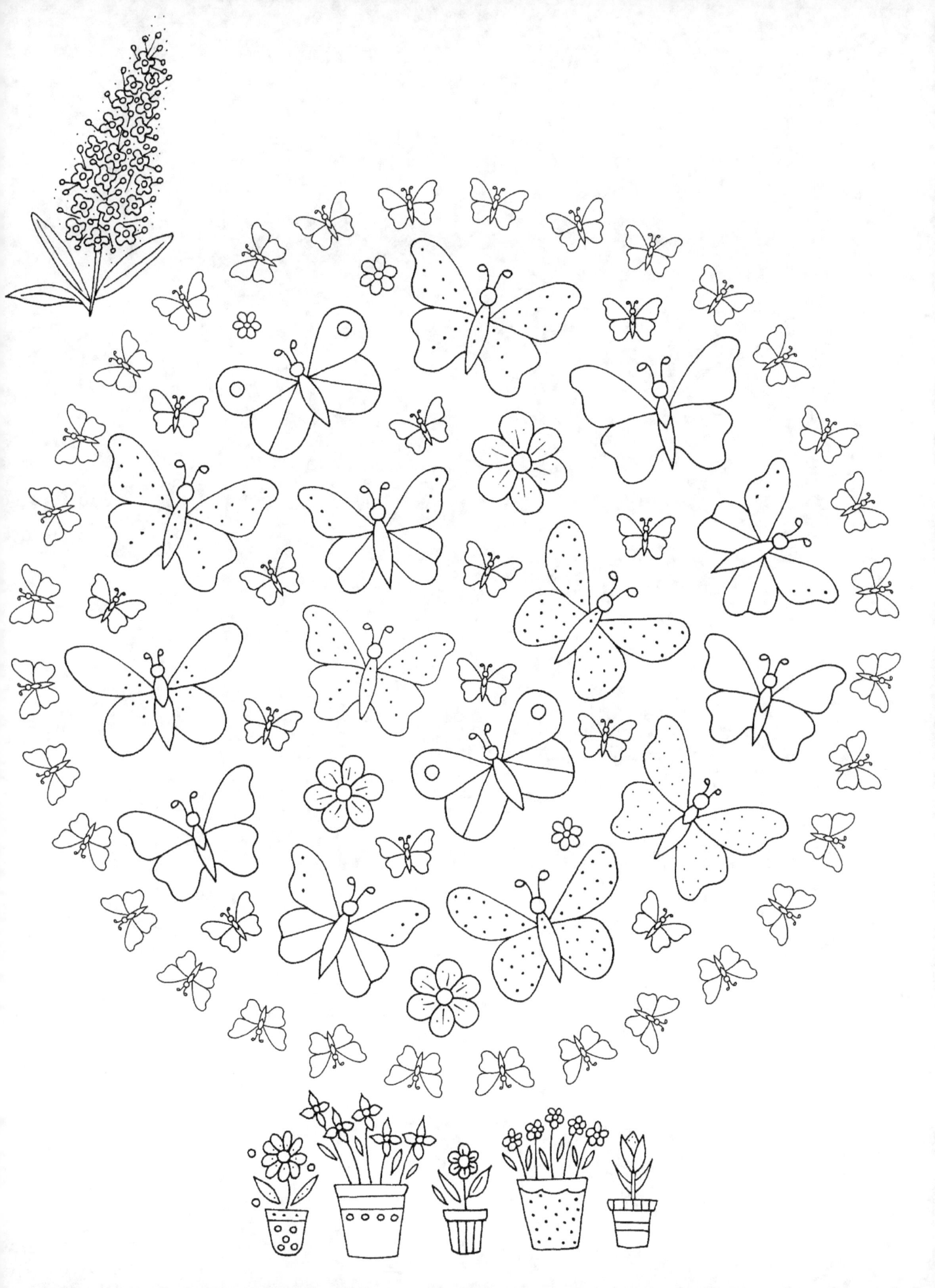

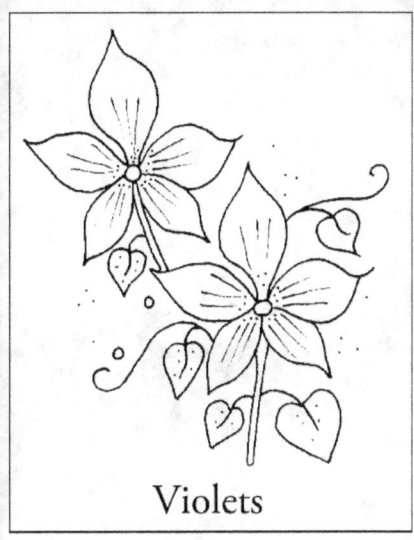

Violets

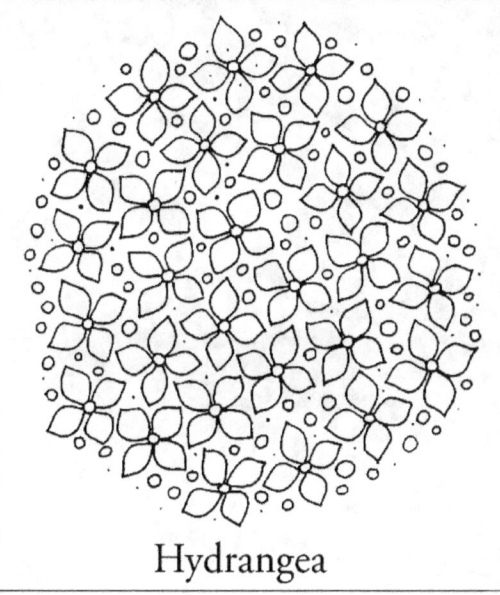

Hydrangea

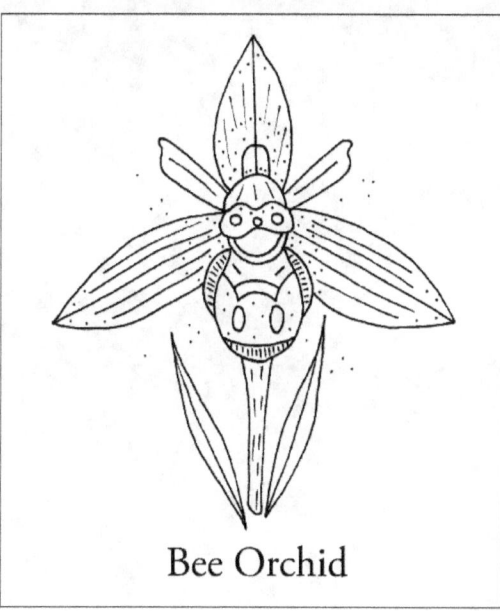

Bee Orchid

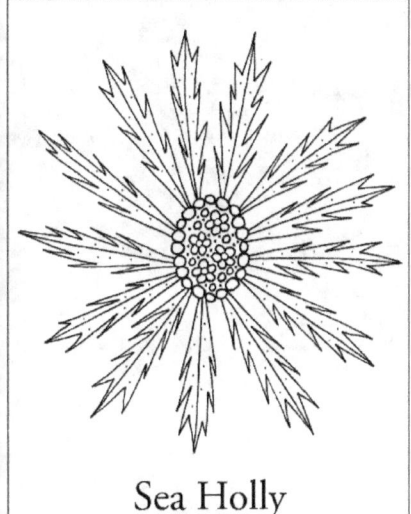

Sea Holly

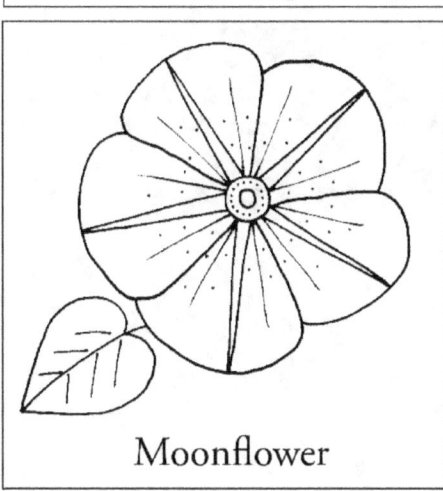

Moonflower

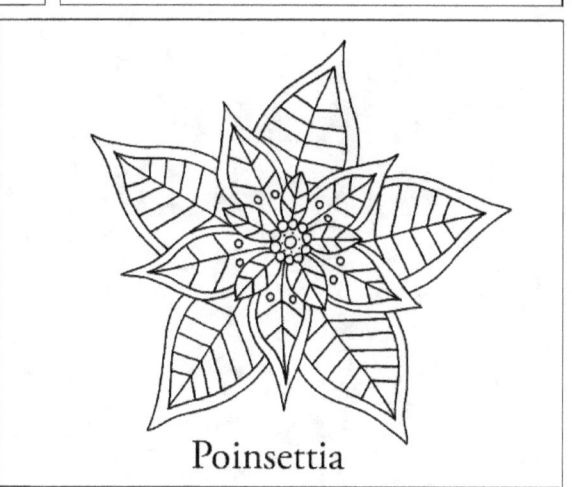

Poinsettia

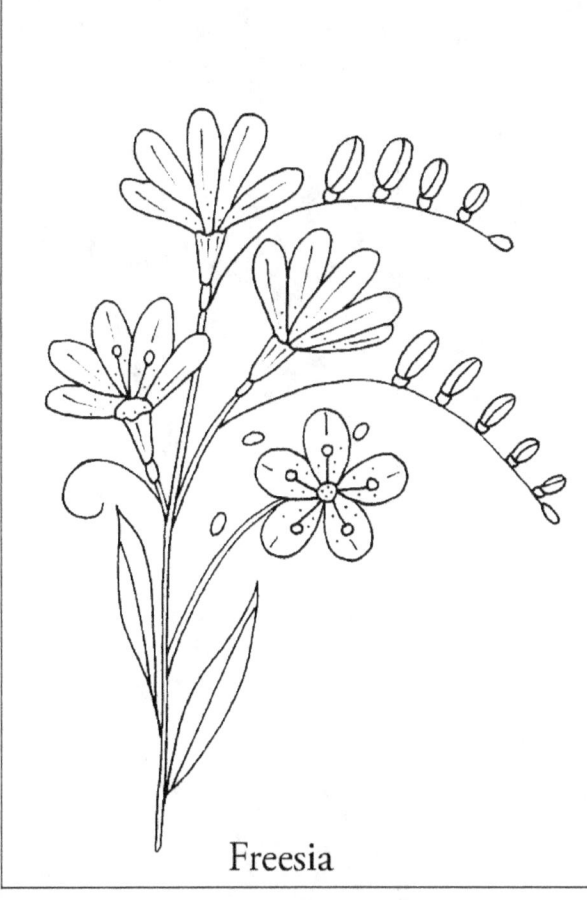

Freesia

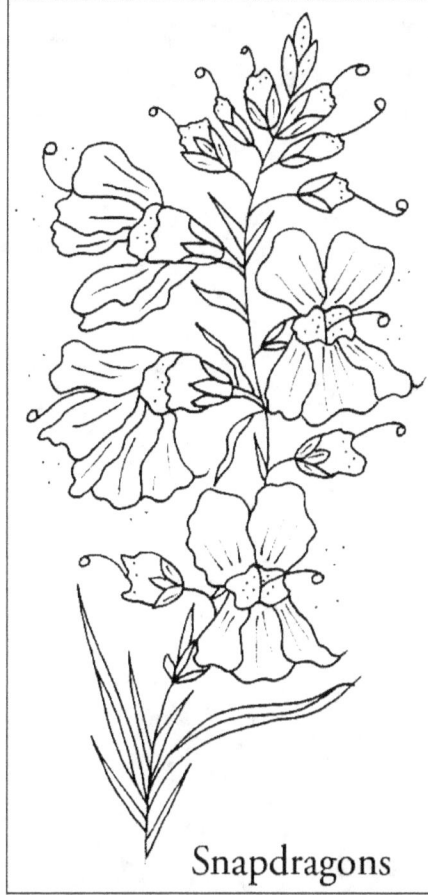

Snapdragons

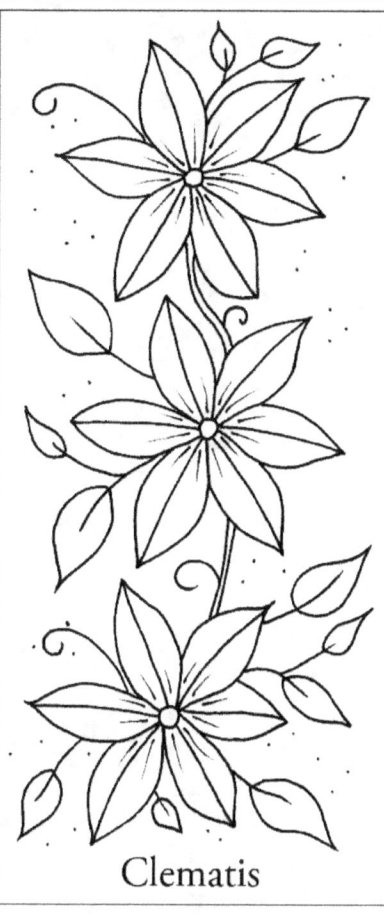

Clematis

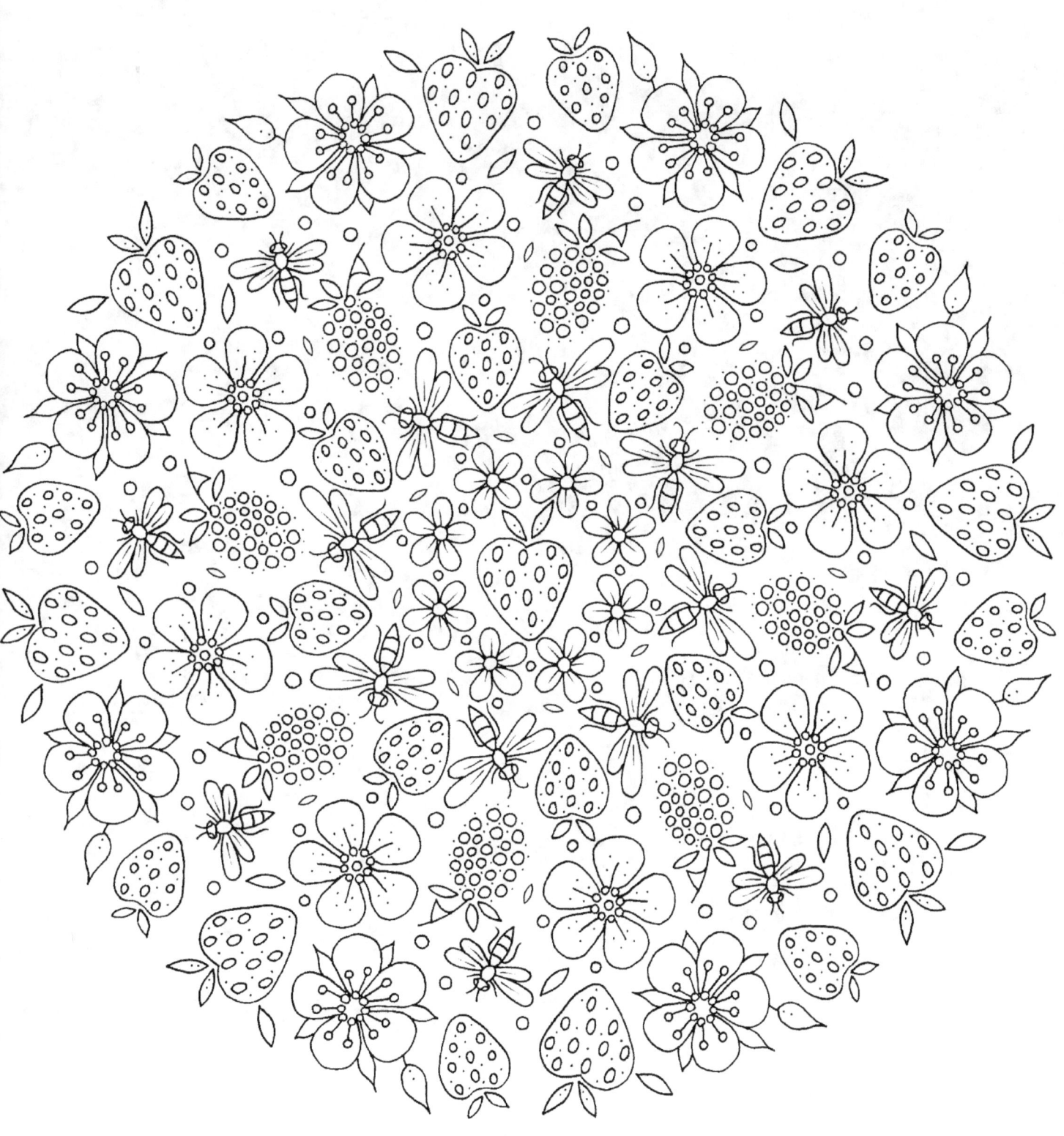

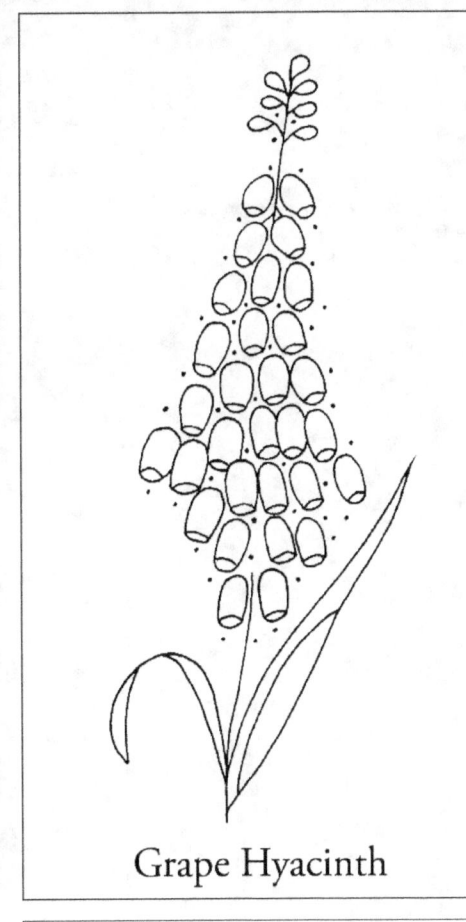

Grape Hyacinth

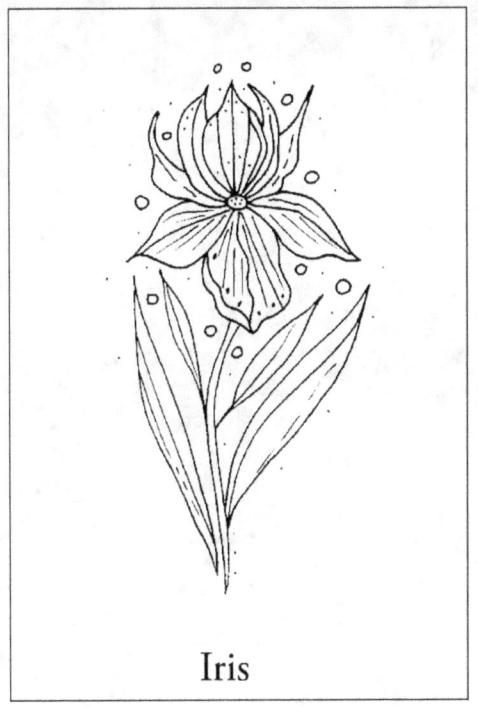

Iris

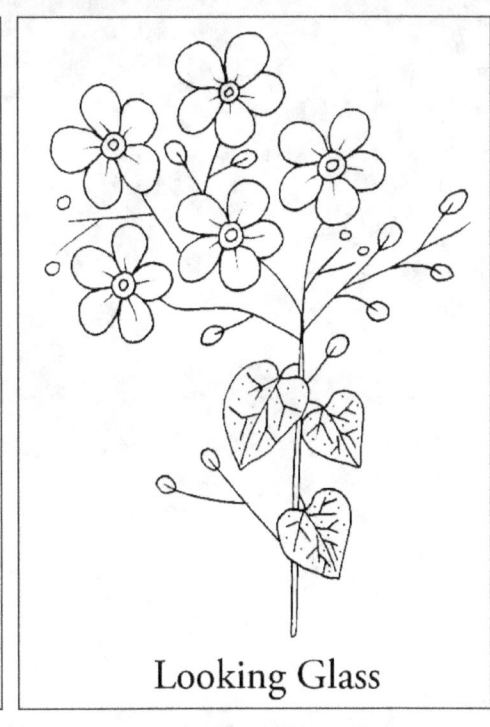

Looking Glass

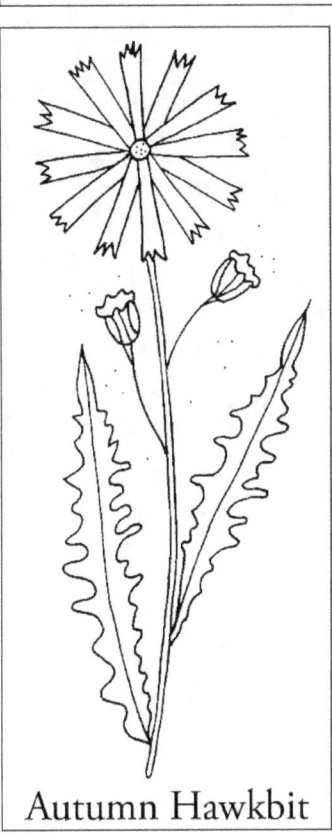

Autumn Hawkbit

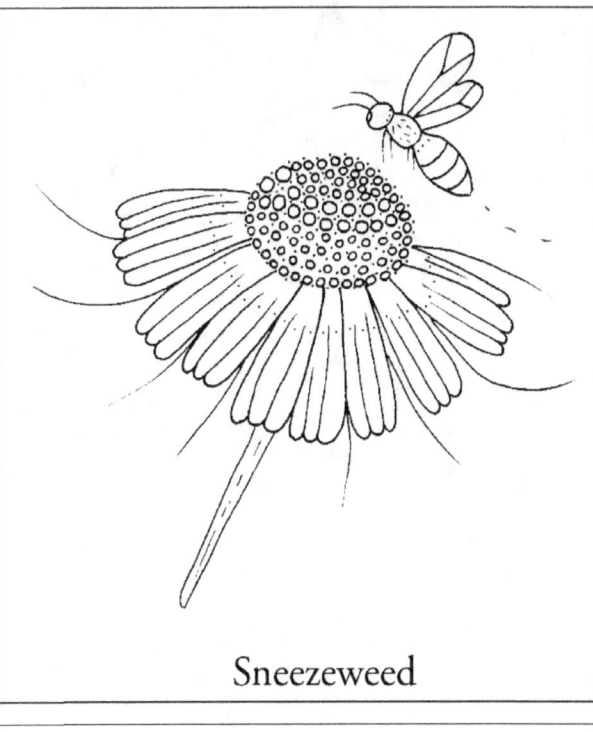

Sneezeweed

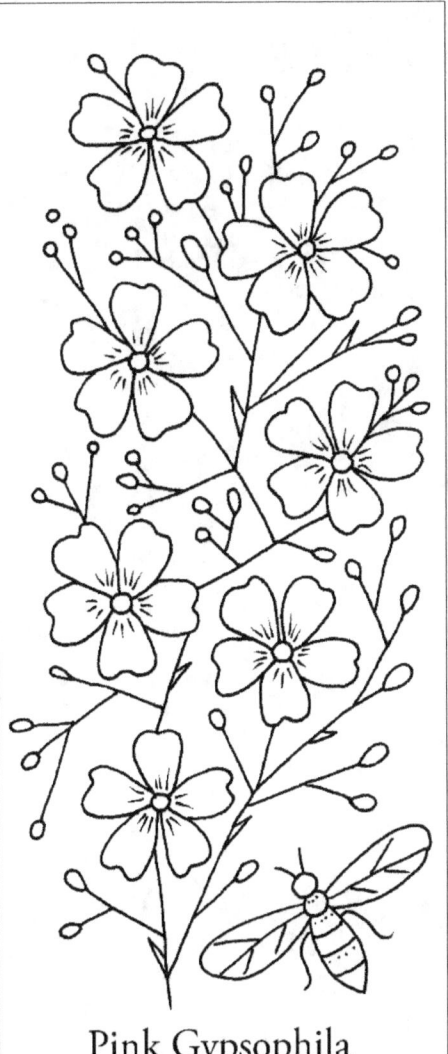

Pink Gypsophila

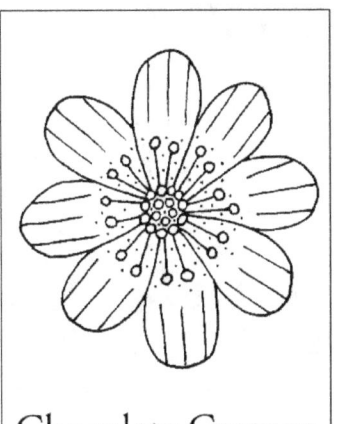

Chocolate Cosmos

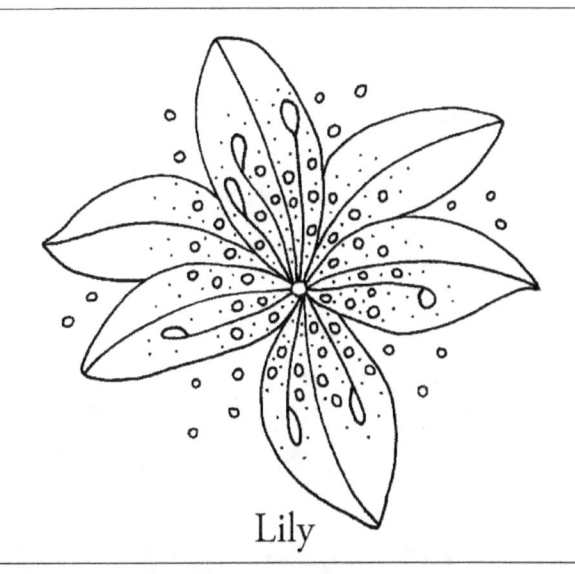

Lily

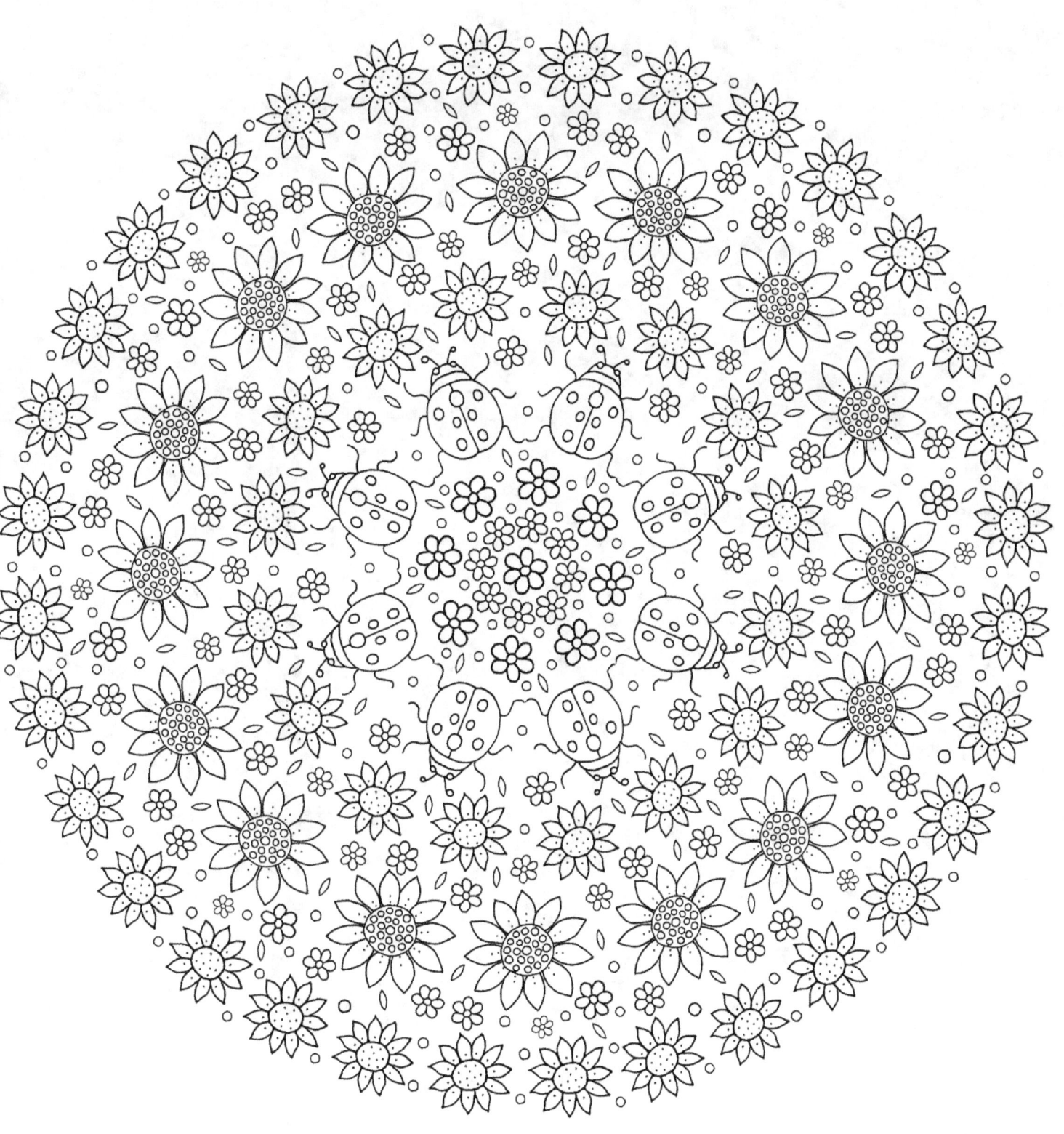

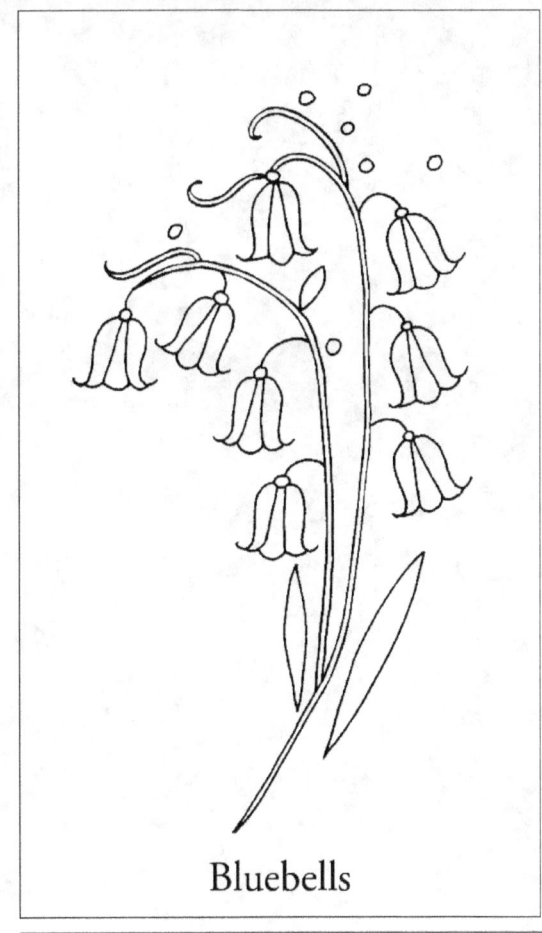

Bluebells

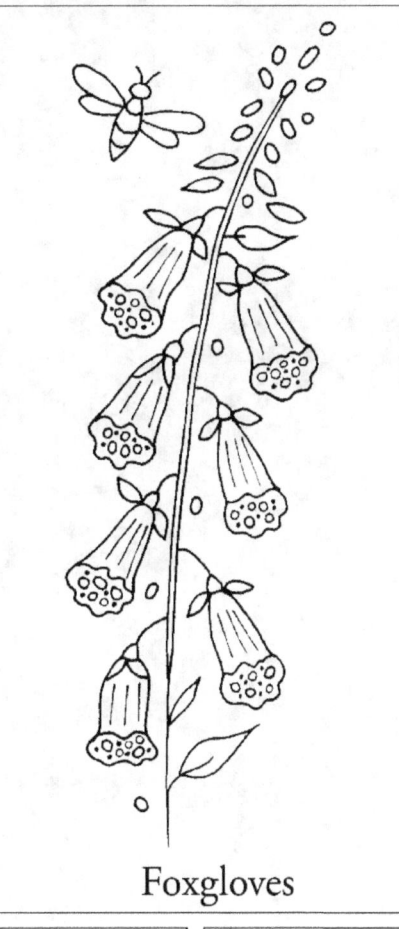

Foxgloves

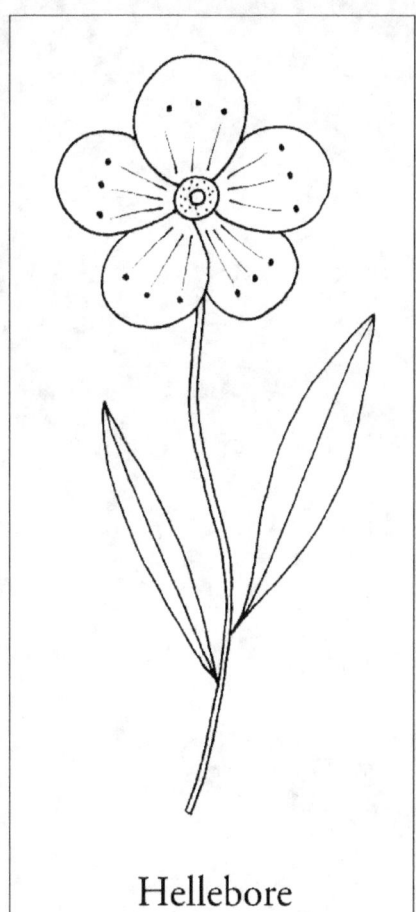

Hellebore

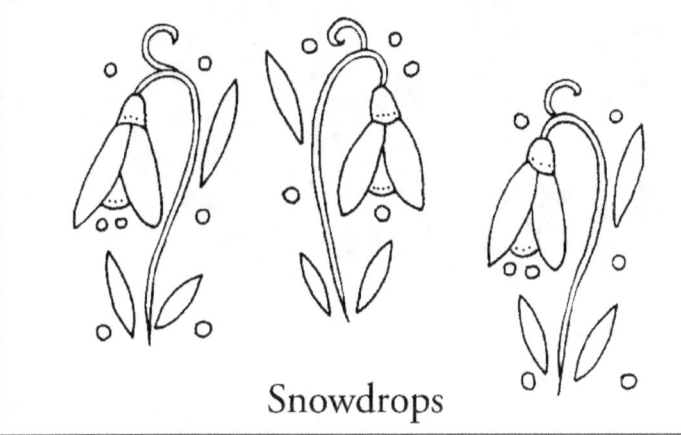

Snowdrops

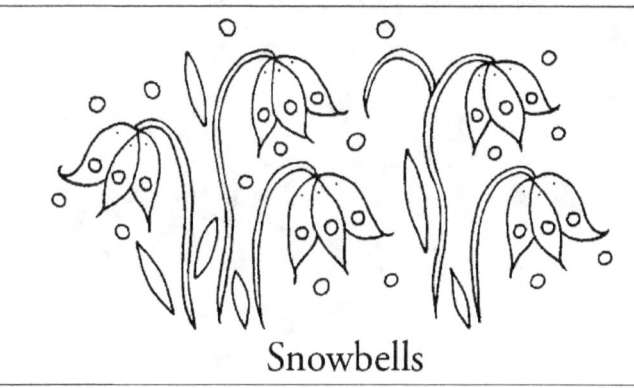

Snowbells

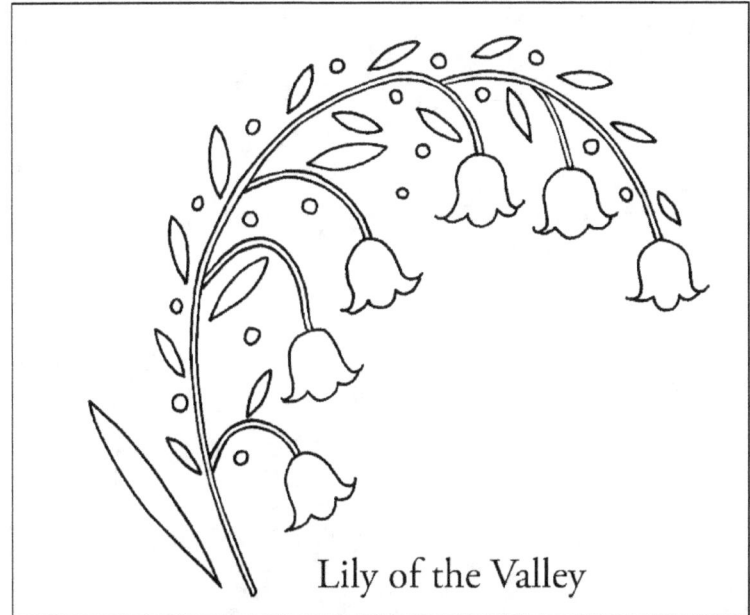

Lily of the Valley

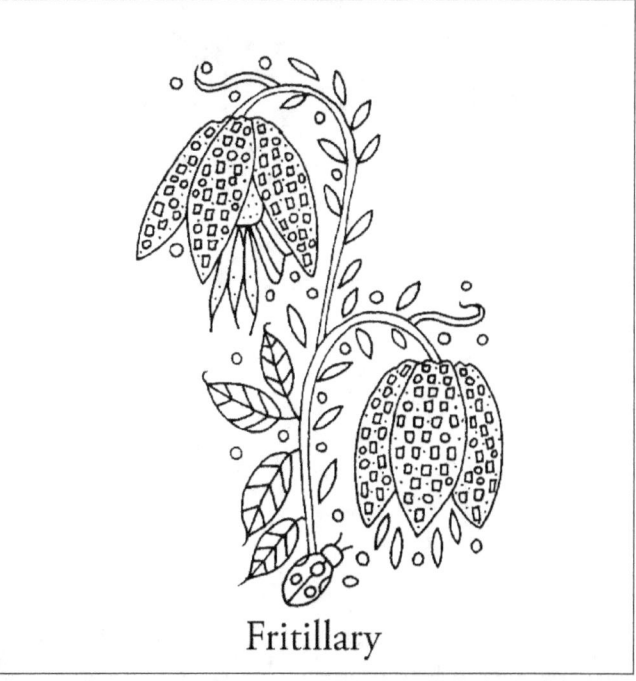

Fritillary

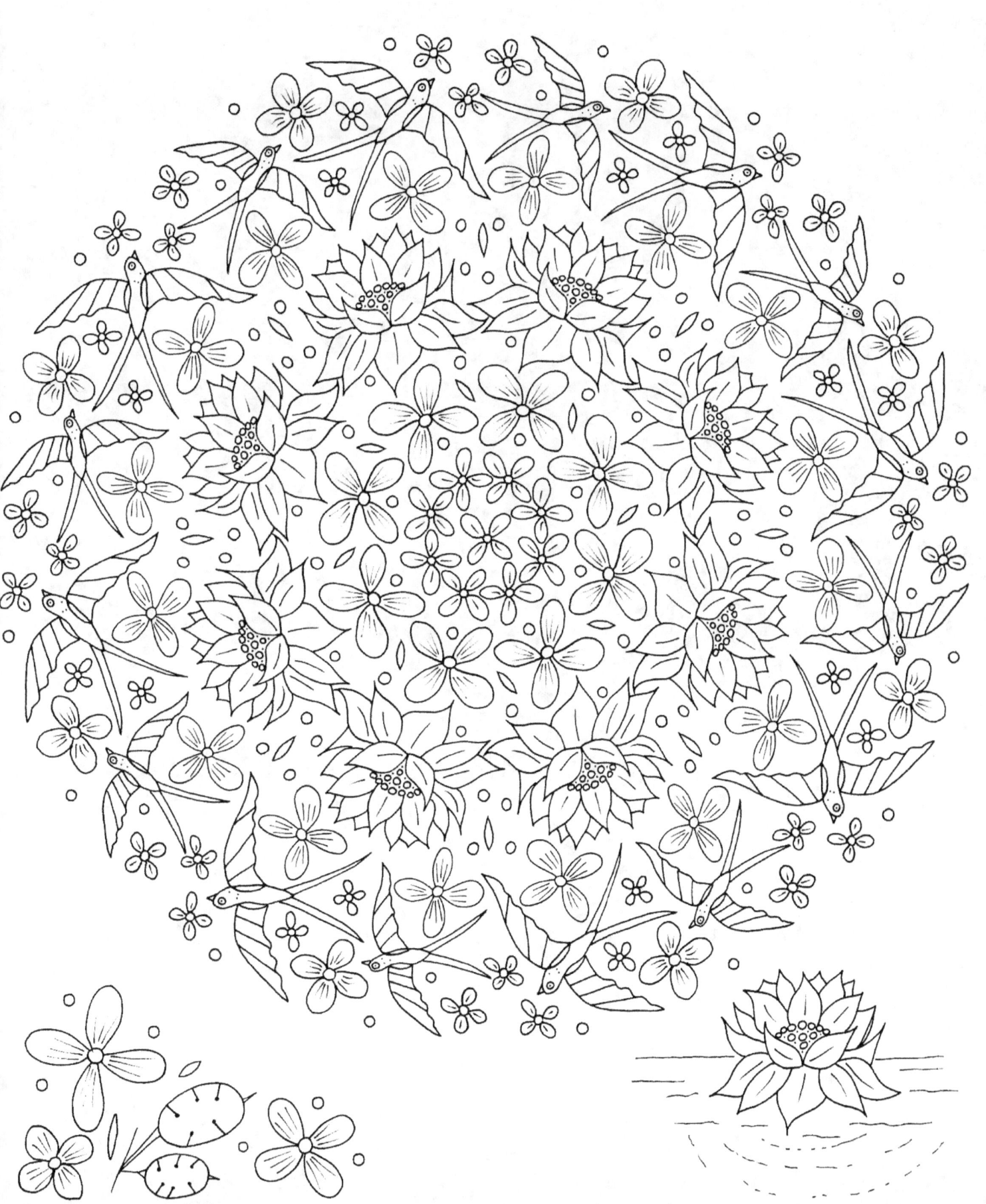

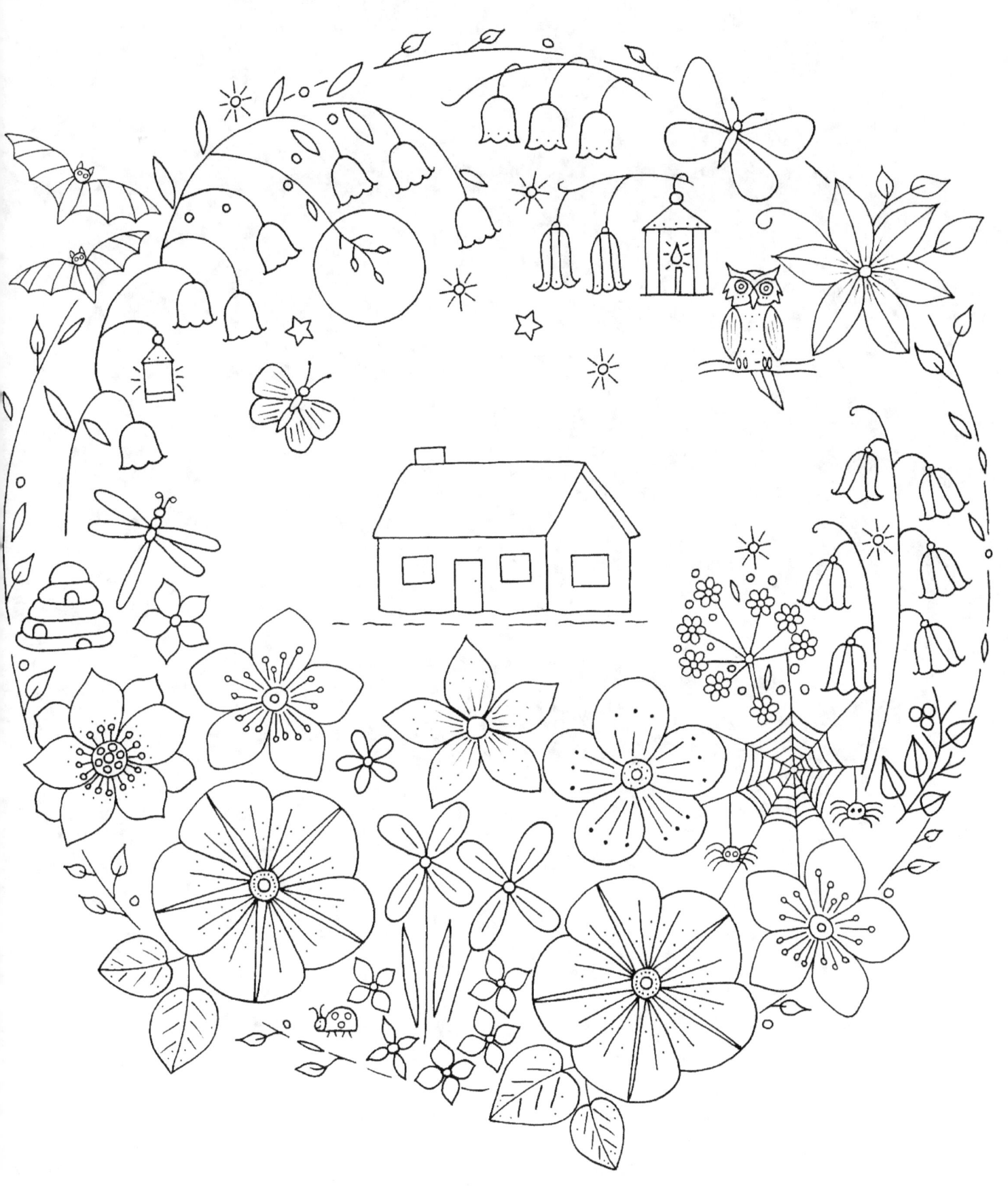

www.ingramcontent.com/pod-product-compliance
Lightning Source LLC
Chambersburg PA
CBHW081533220526
45467CB00010B/3174